Mindfulness
Therapy

30 PAGES

All rights reserved. This book or any portion thereof may not be reproduced or used in any manner whatsoever without the express written permission of the publisher except for the use of brief quotations in a book review or scholarly journal.

First Printing: 2024
QuanTTum Healing

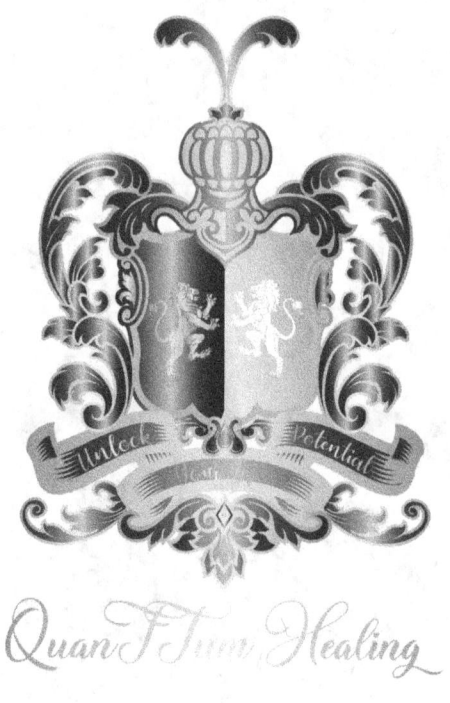

Copyright © 2024 by QuanTTum Healing

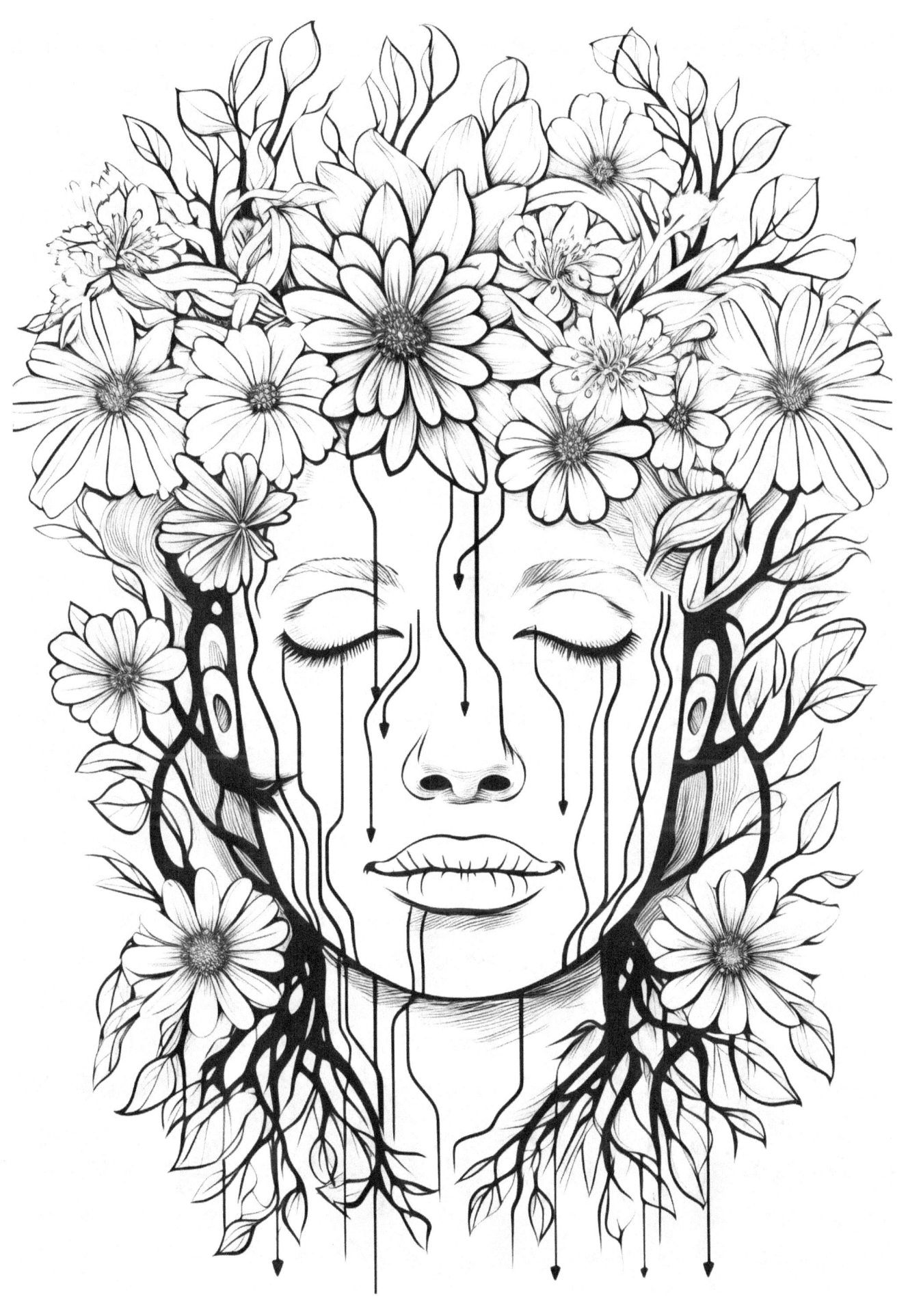

I am doing the BEST you can

I am WORTHY and LOVABLE

It's OK to ask for Help

I am capable of AMAZING thing

E.G. (WRITE NOTE TO SELF AS A REFLECTION AFTER EACH DRAWING)

My boundaries are Important

My FEELINGS are Valid

It's OK to Start Over and TRY AGAIN

I am ALLOWED to say NO

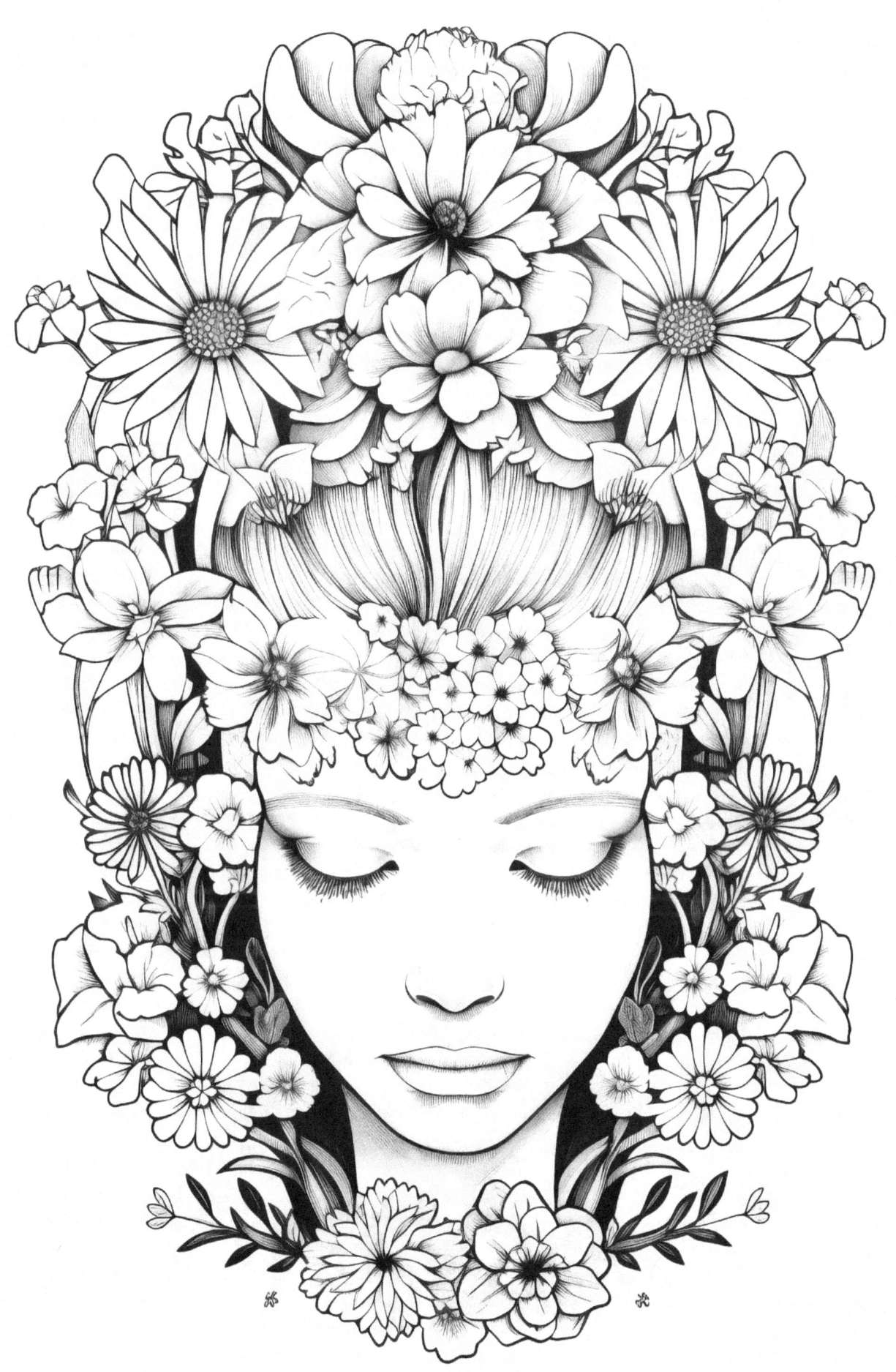

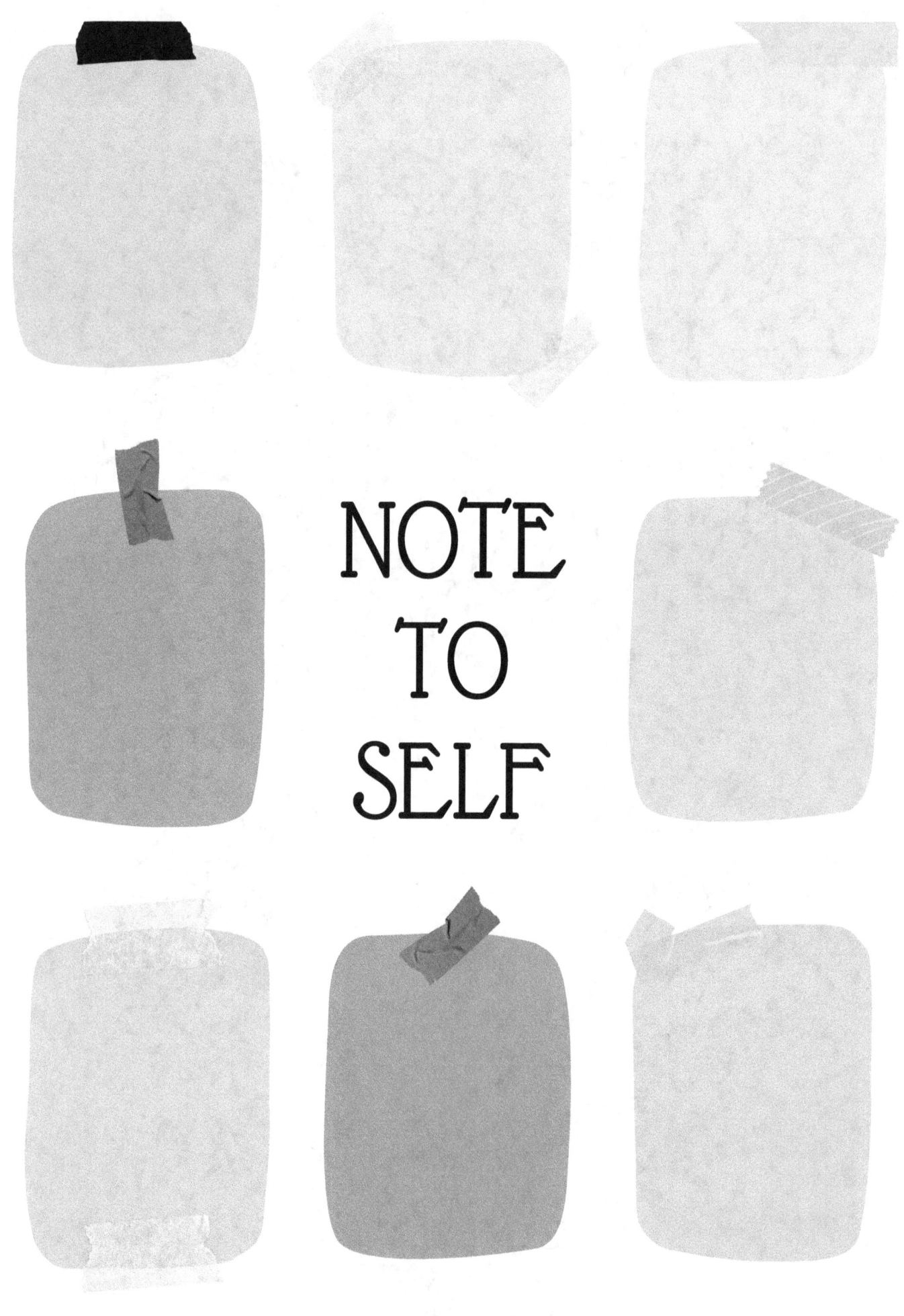

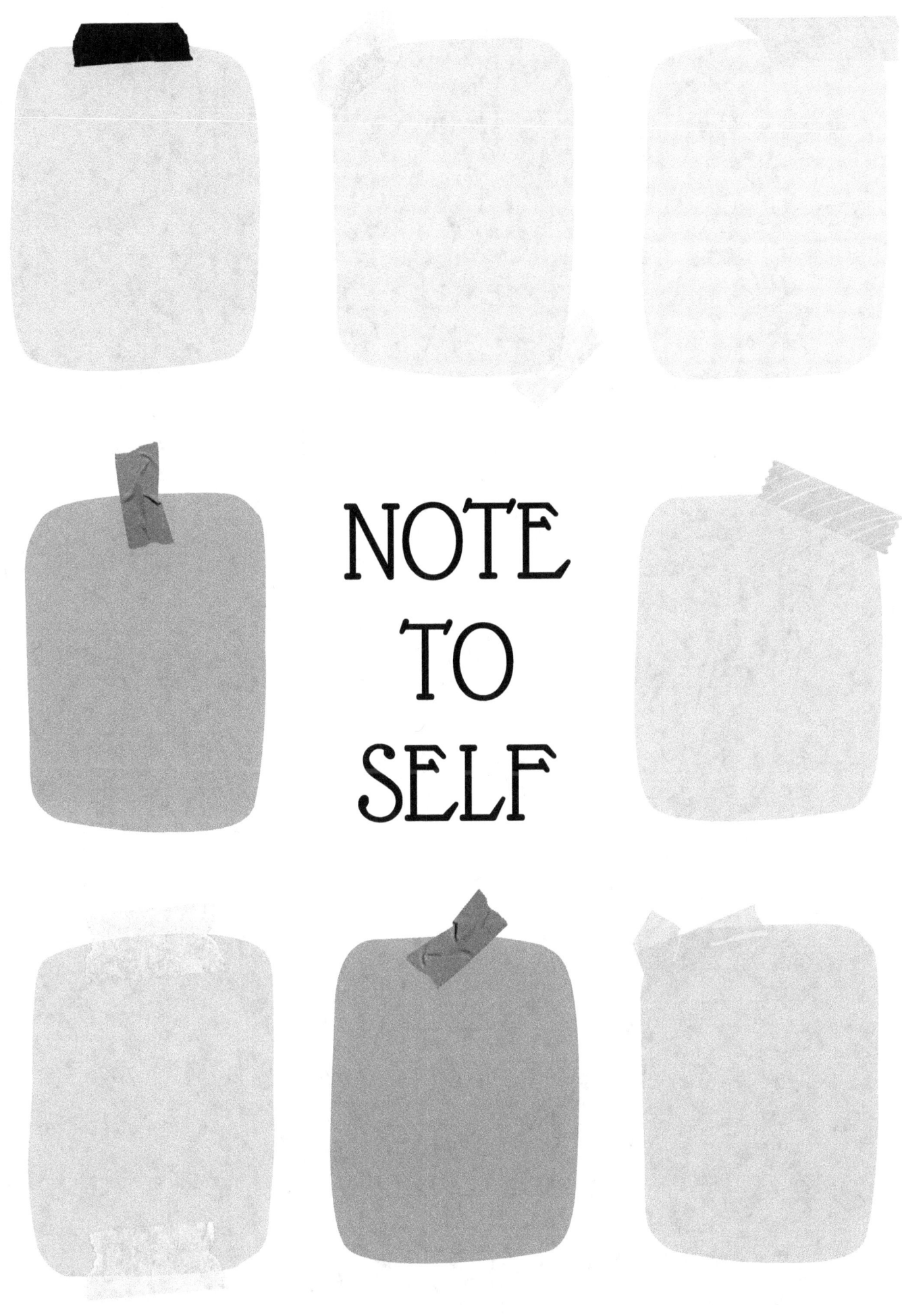

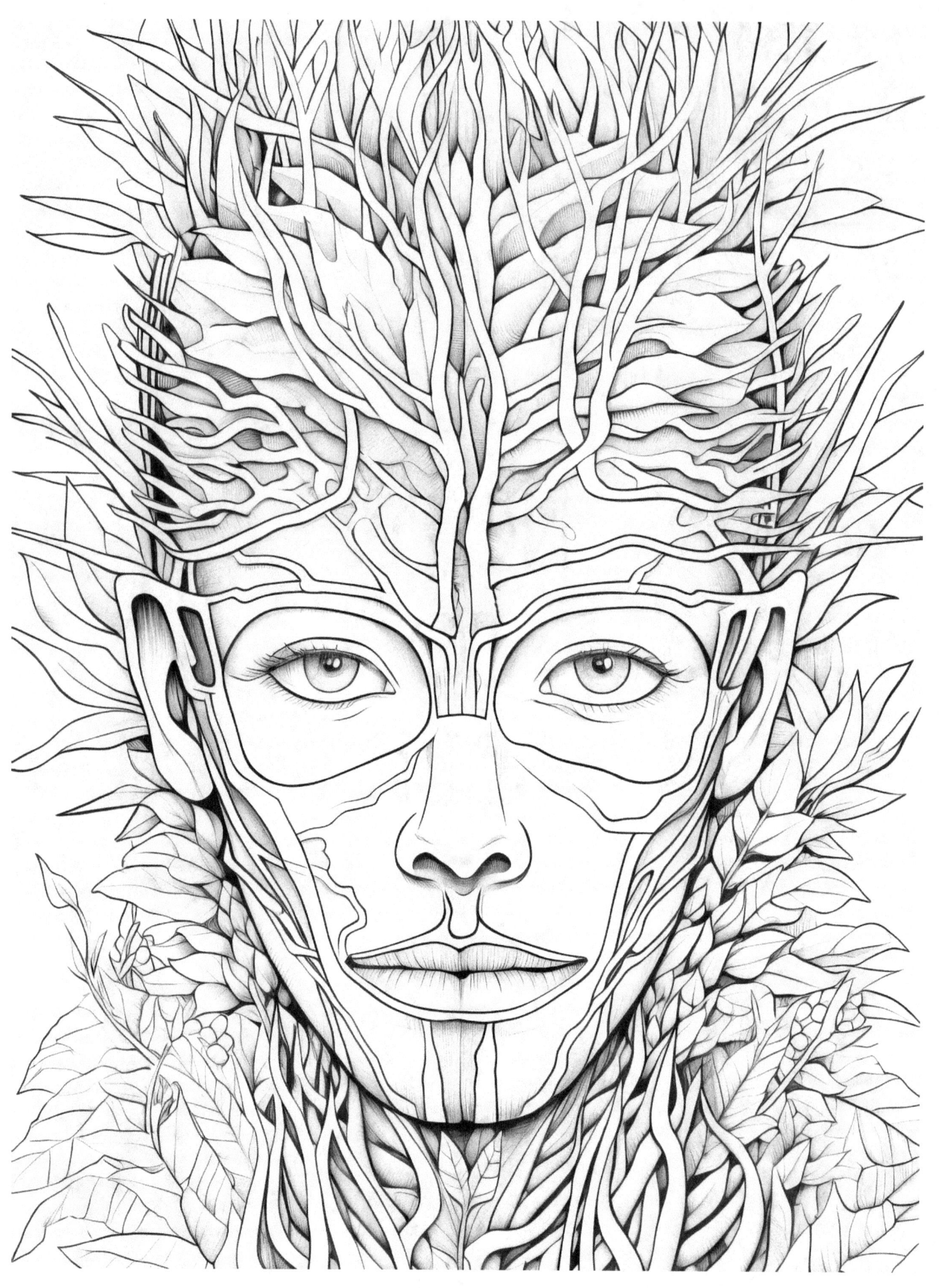

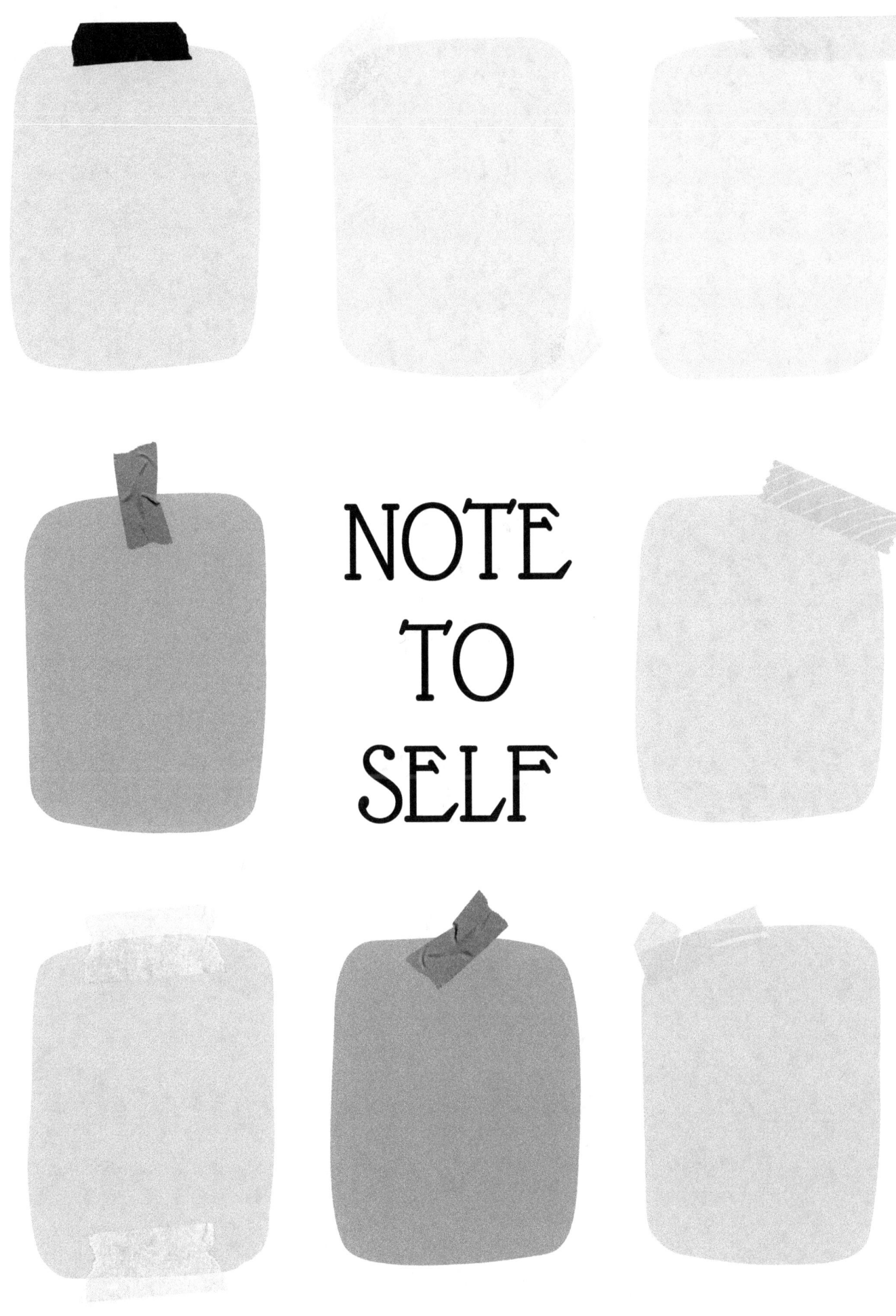

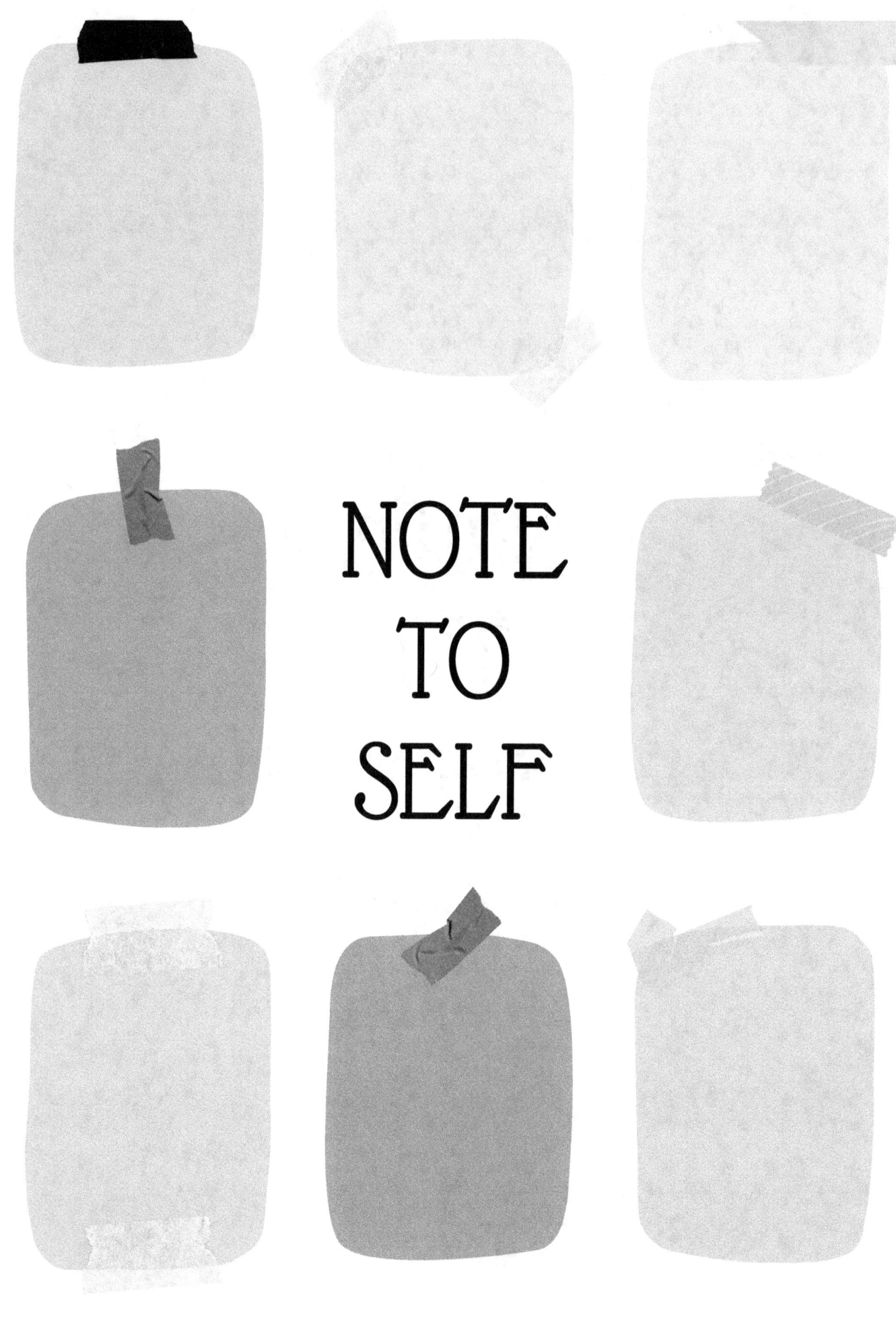

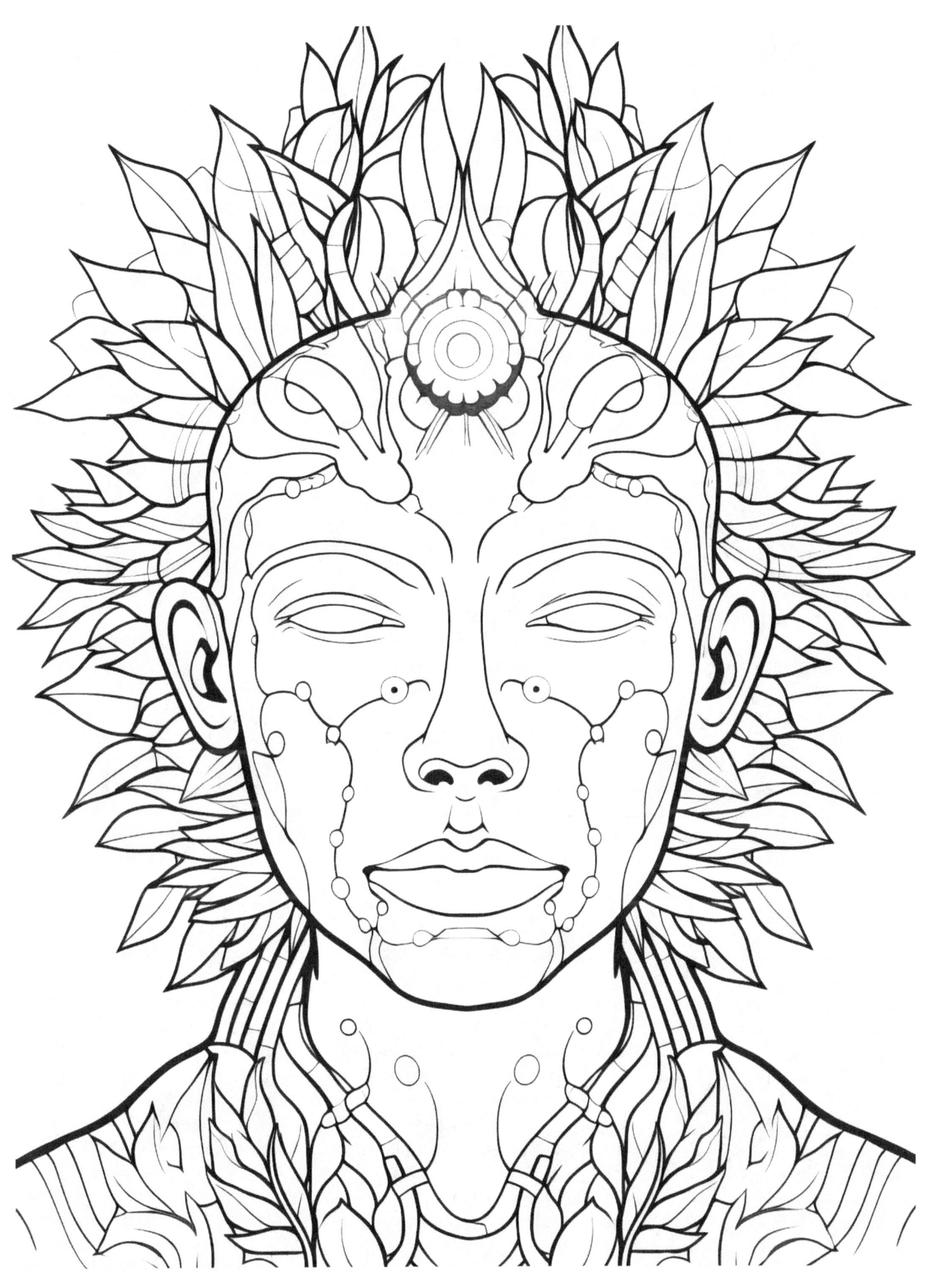

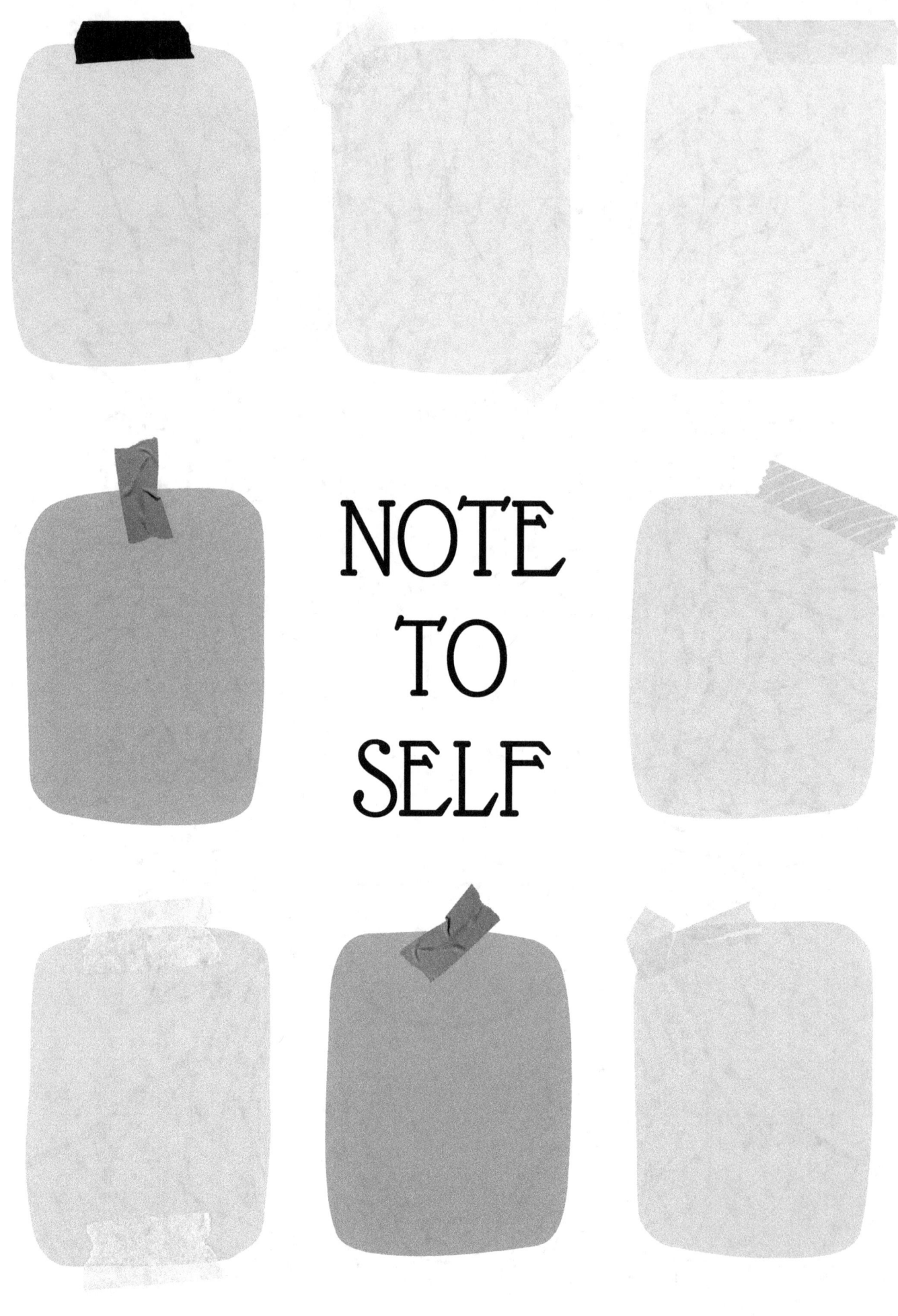

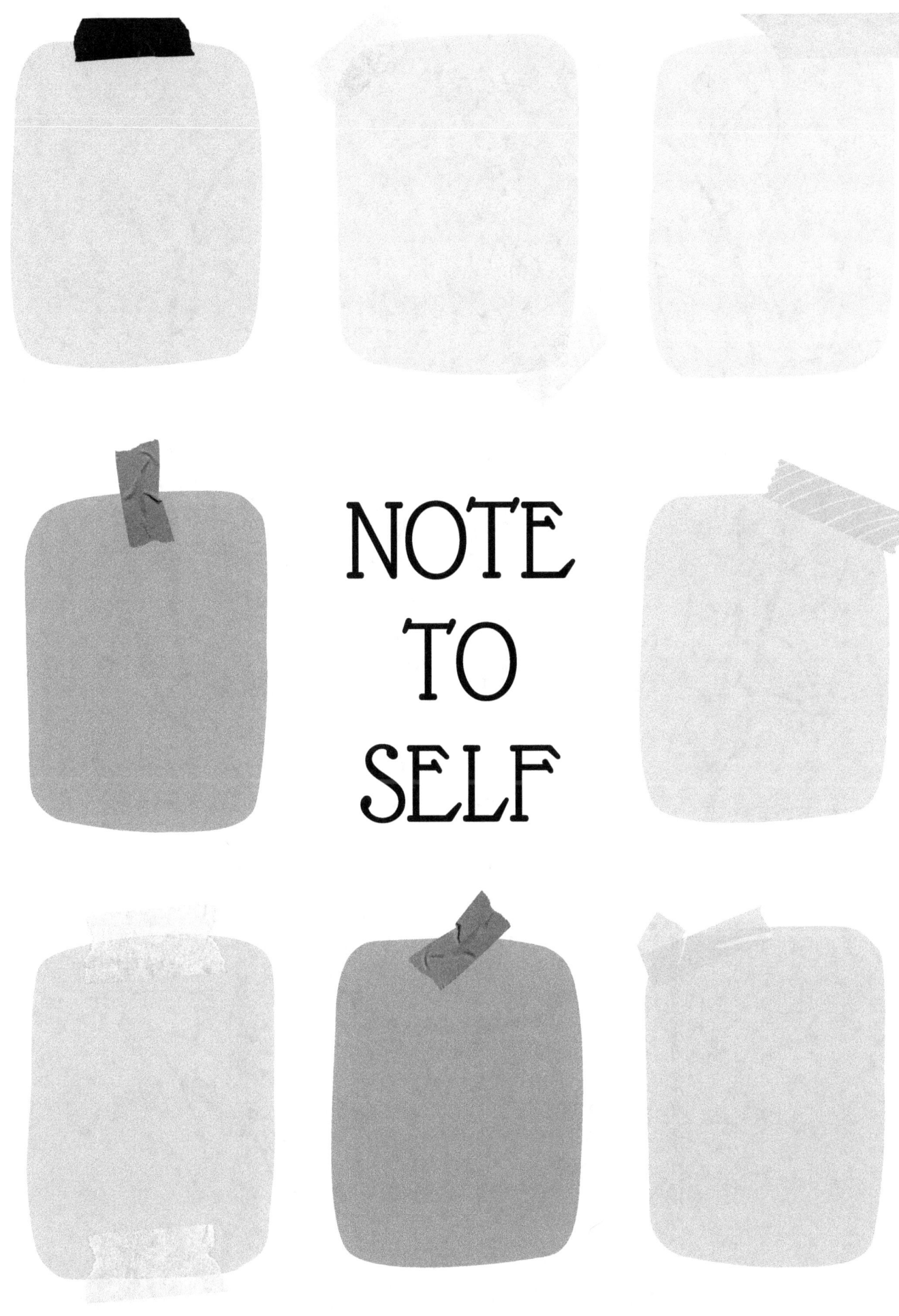

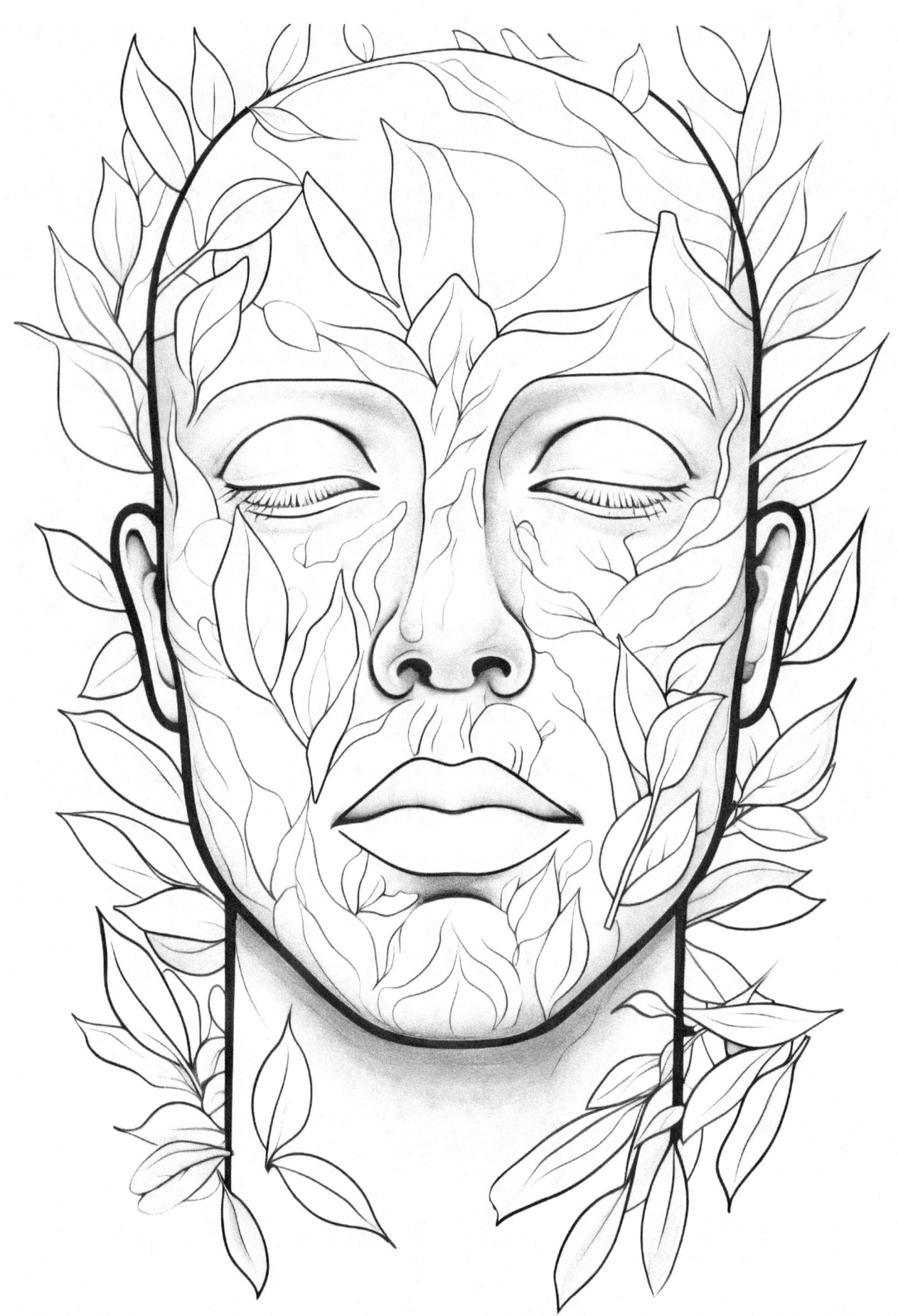

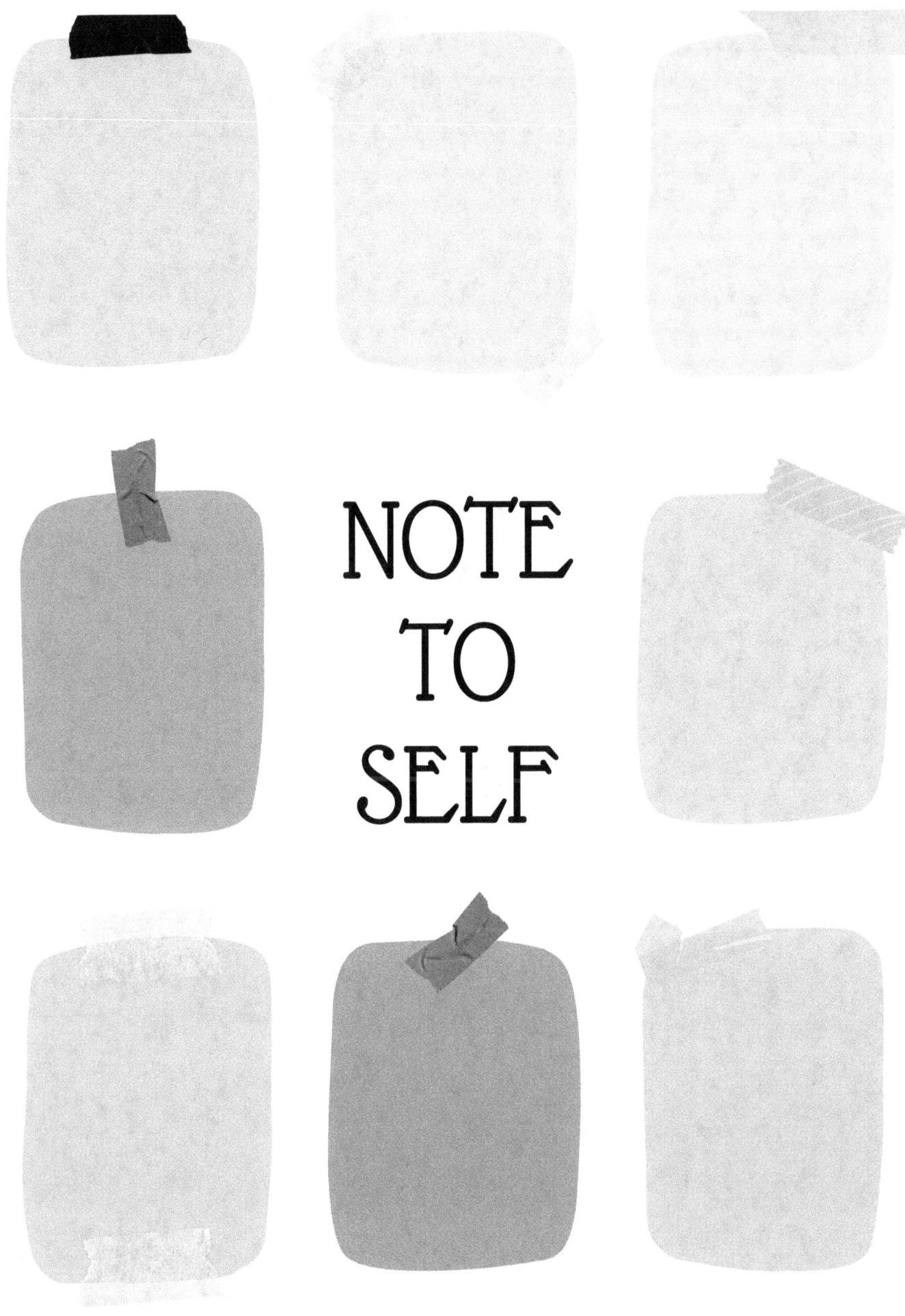

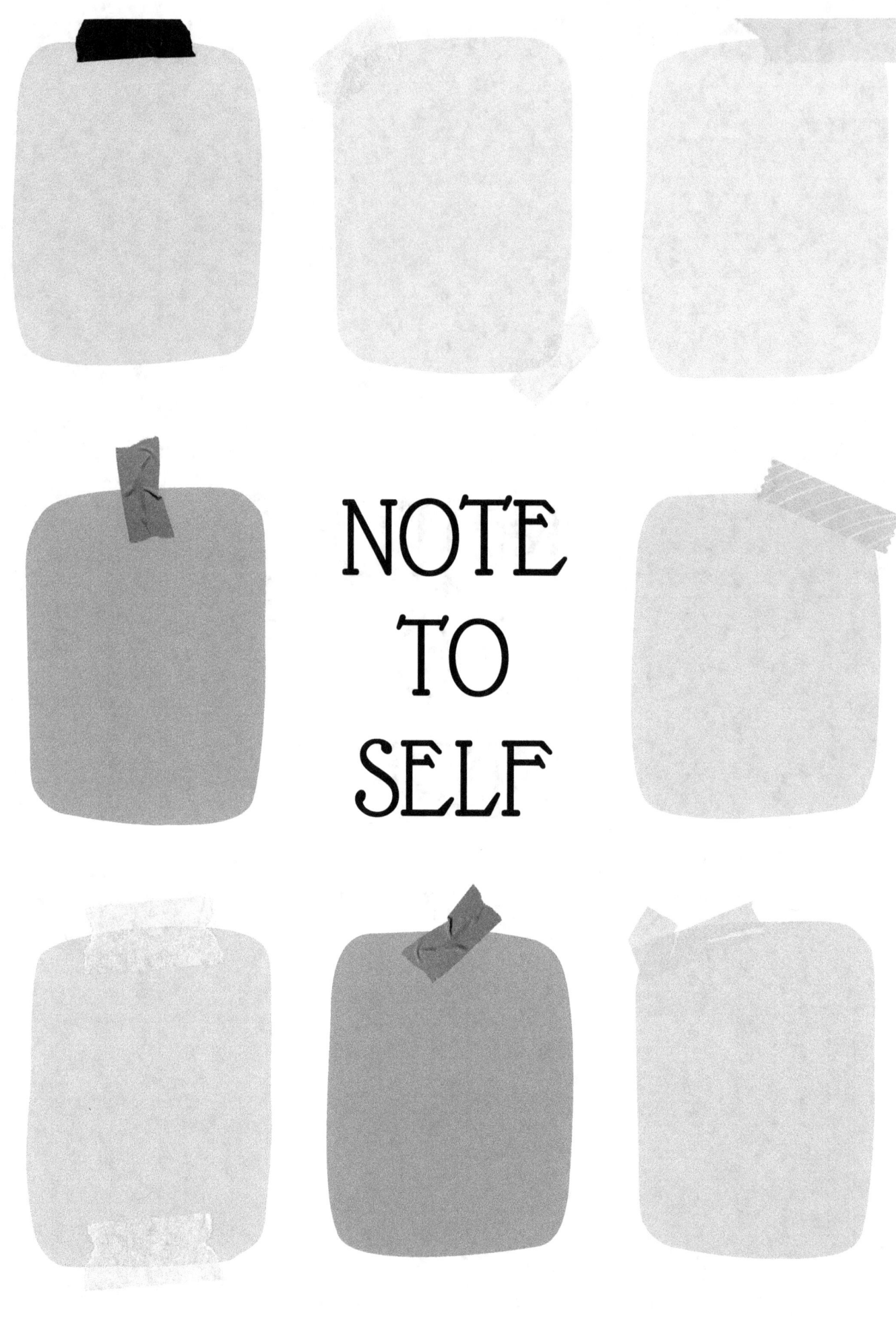

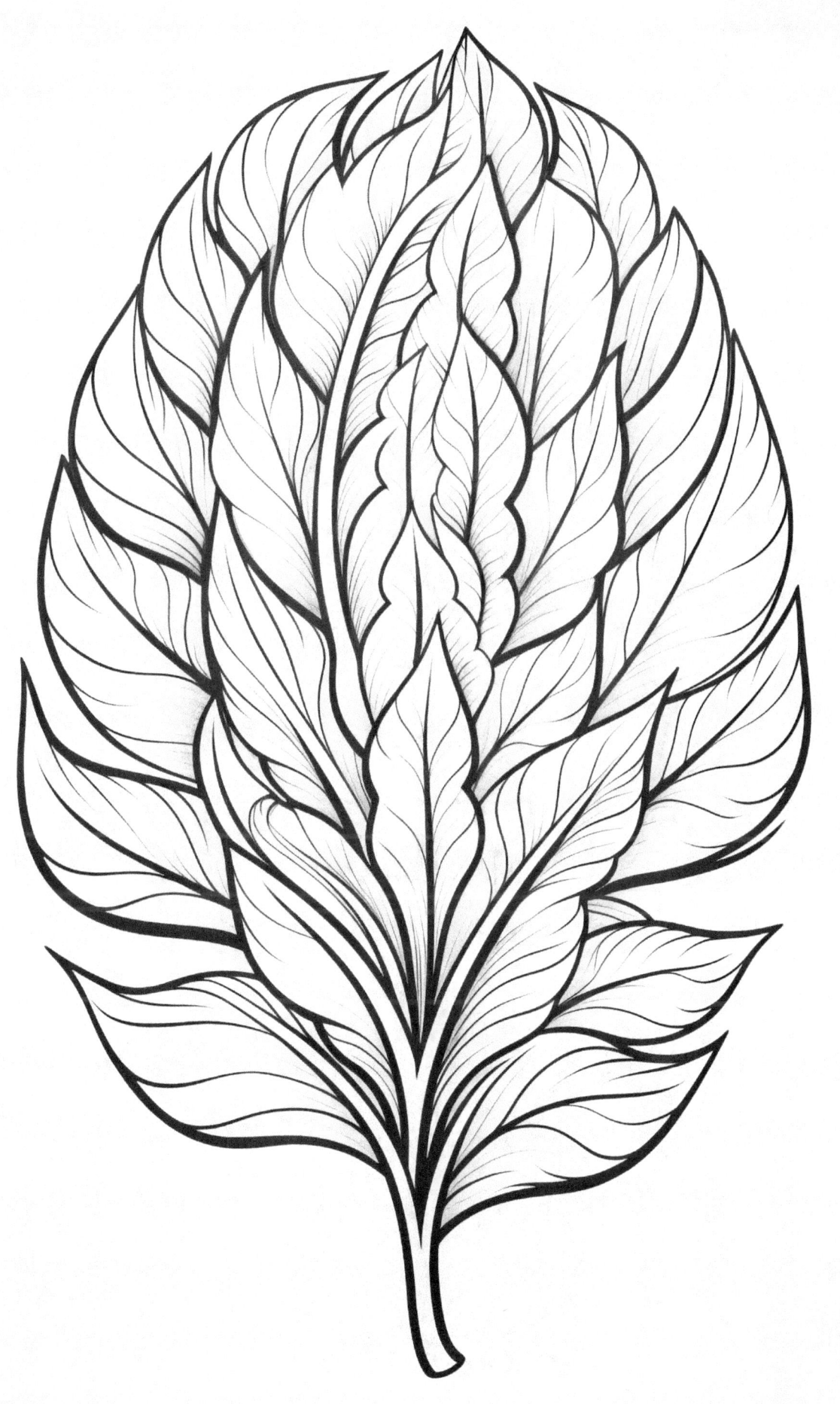

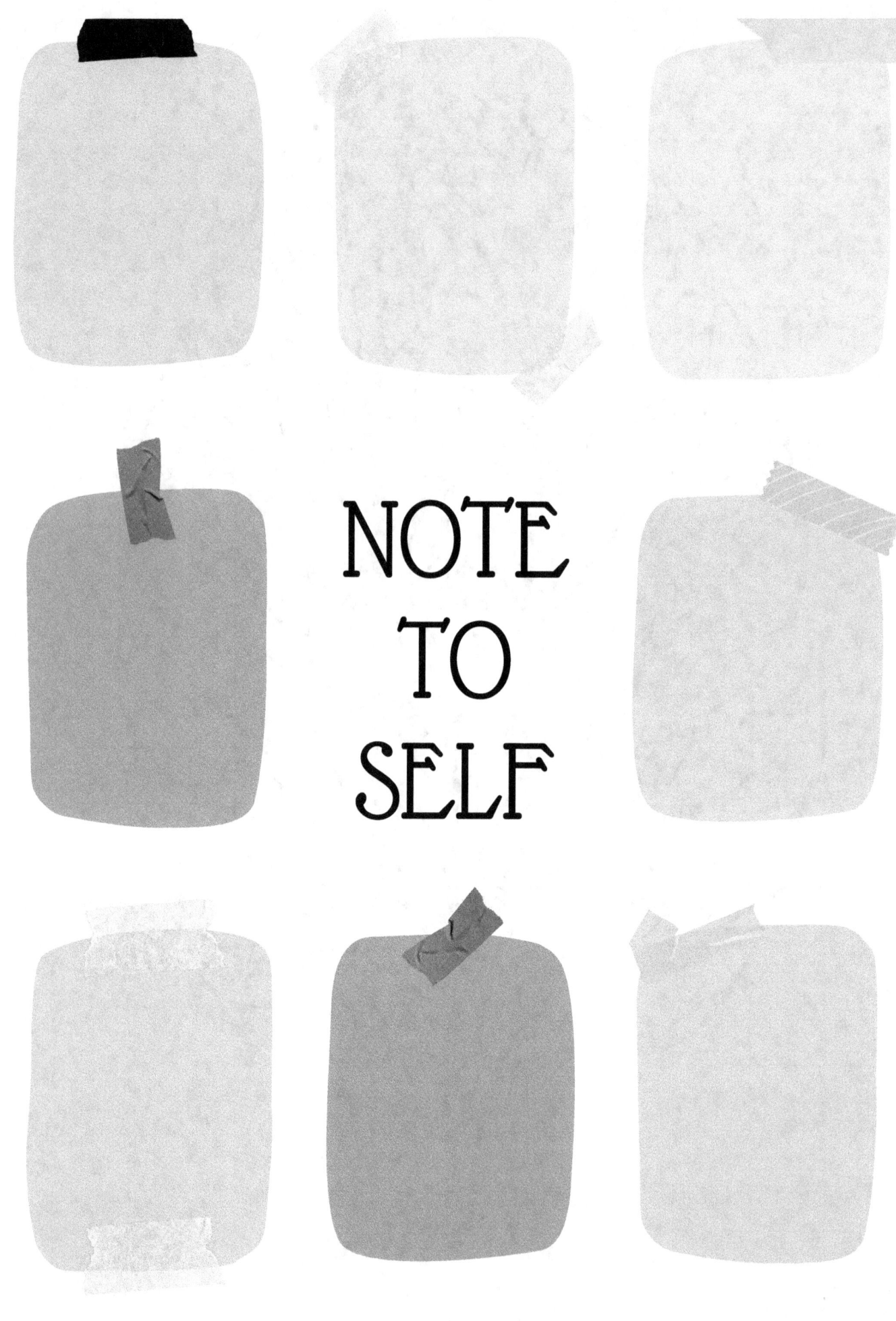

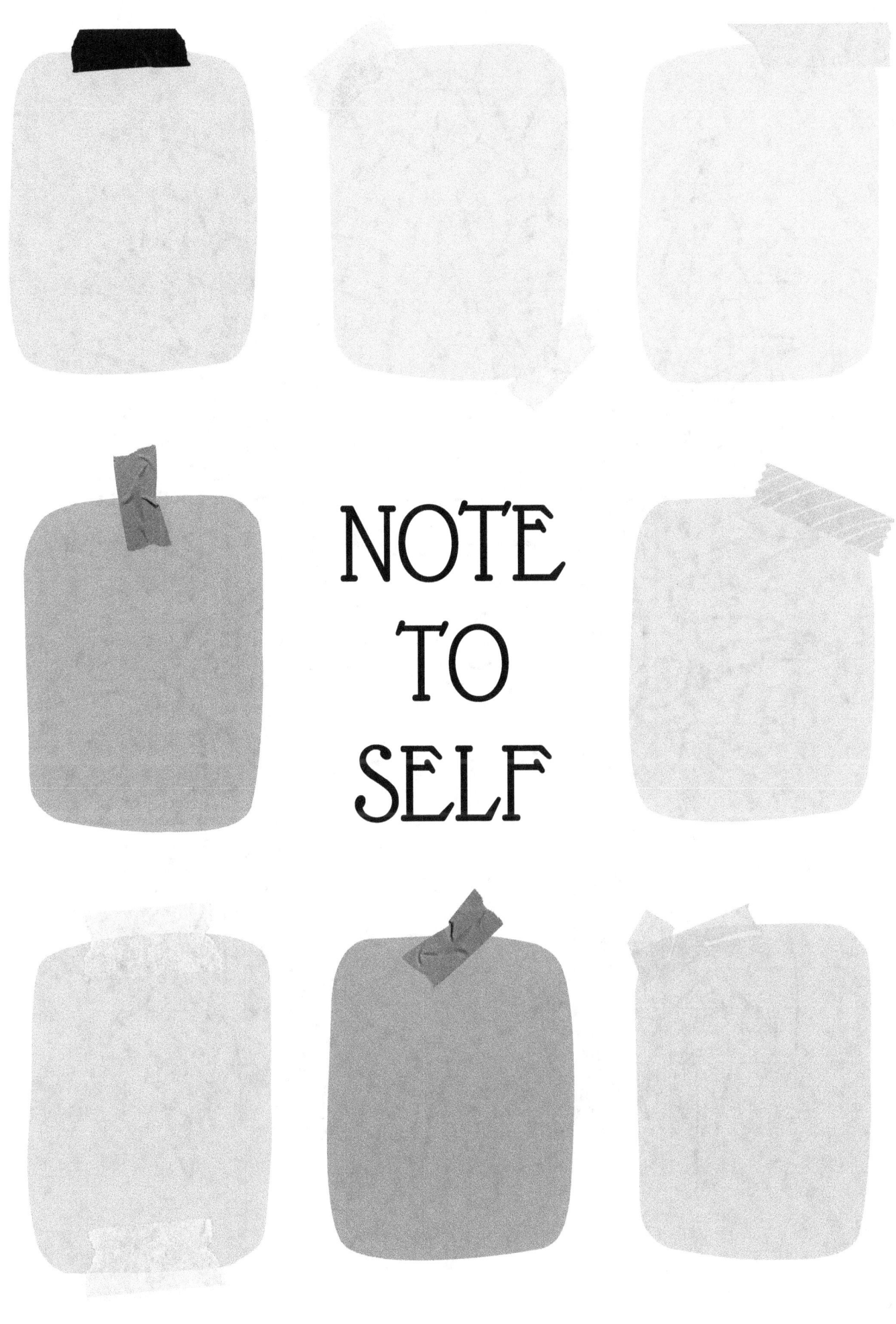

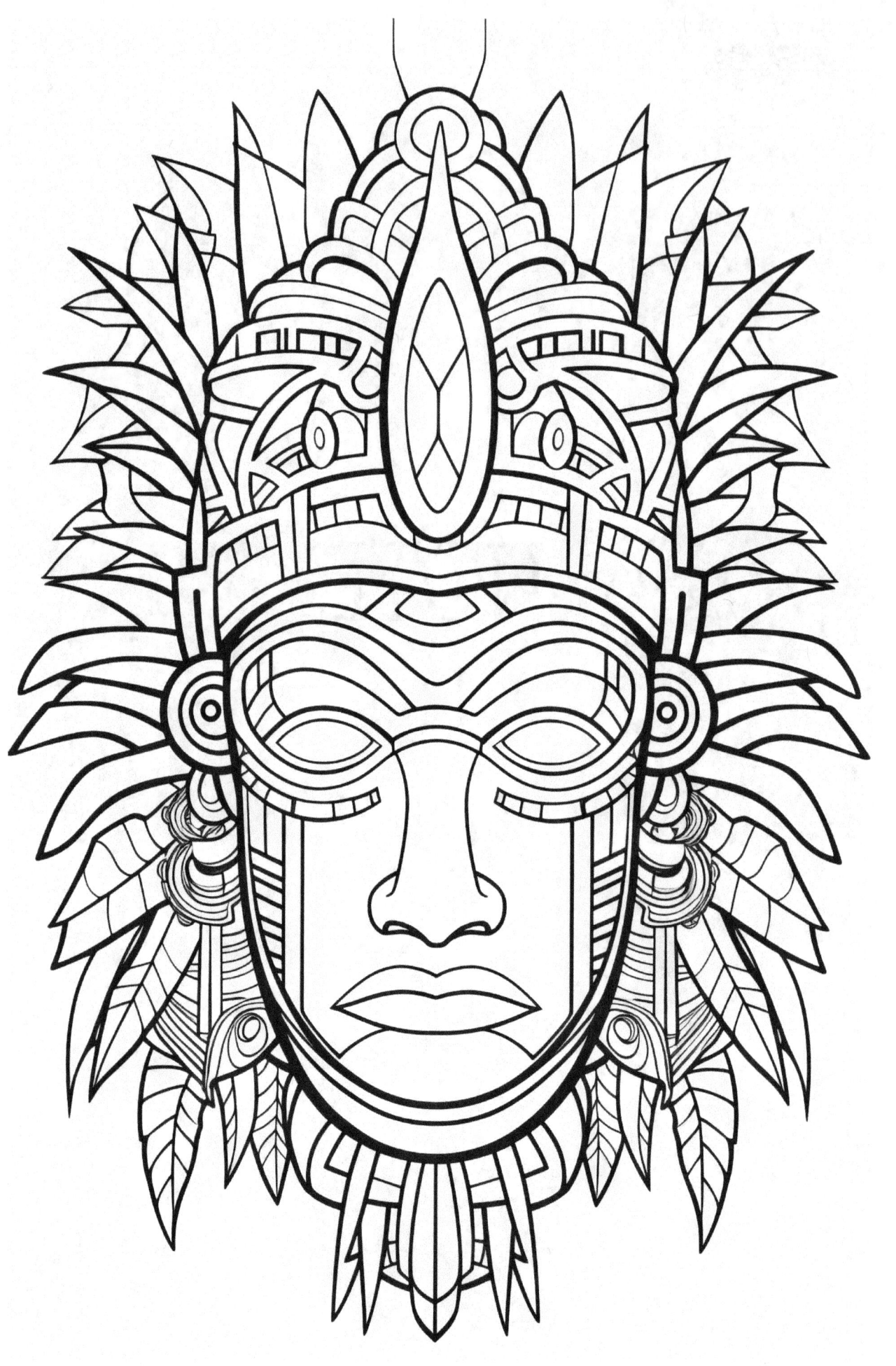

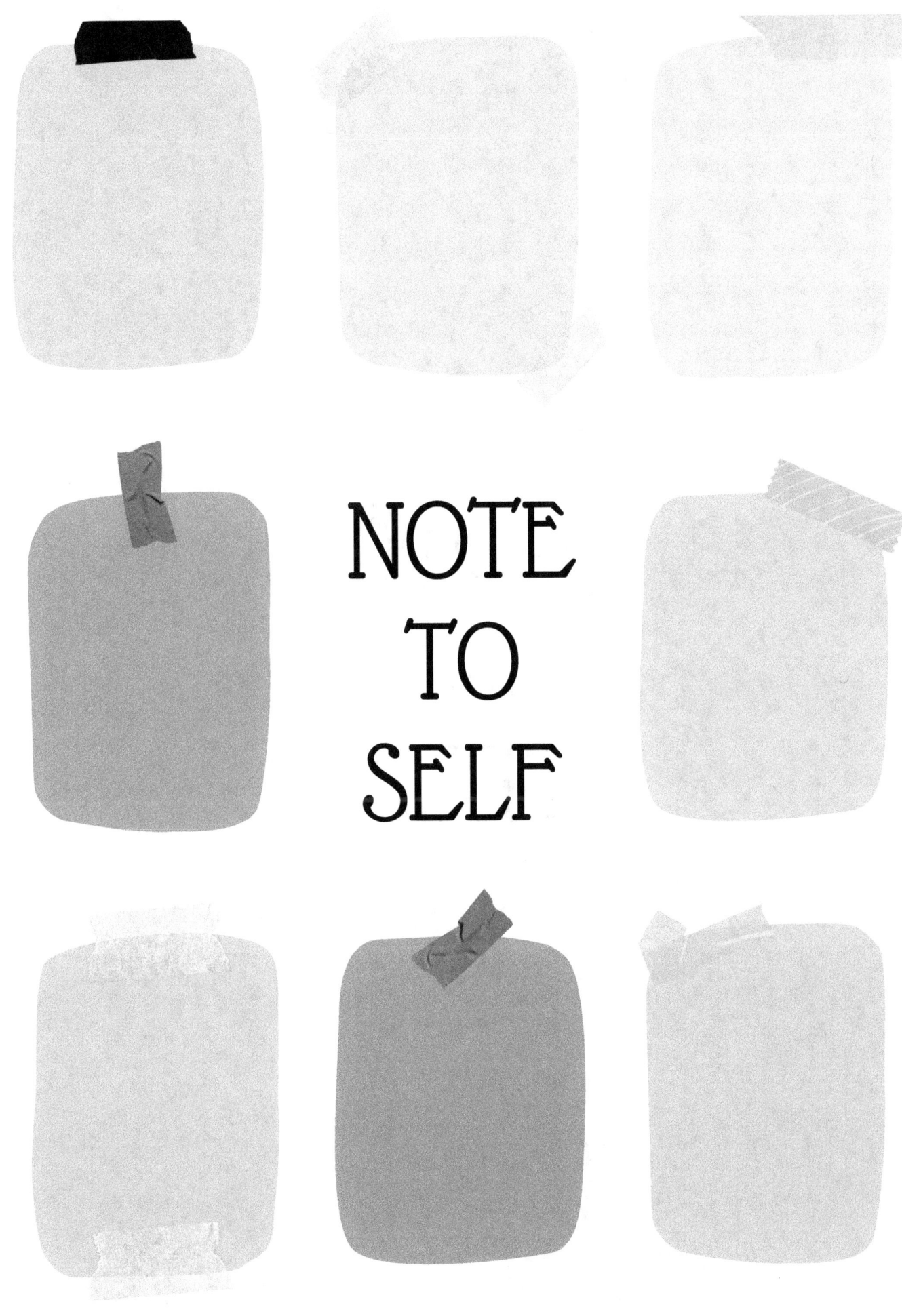

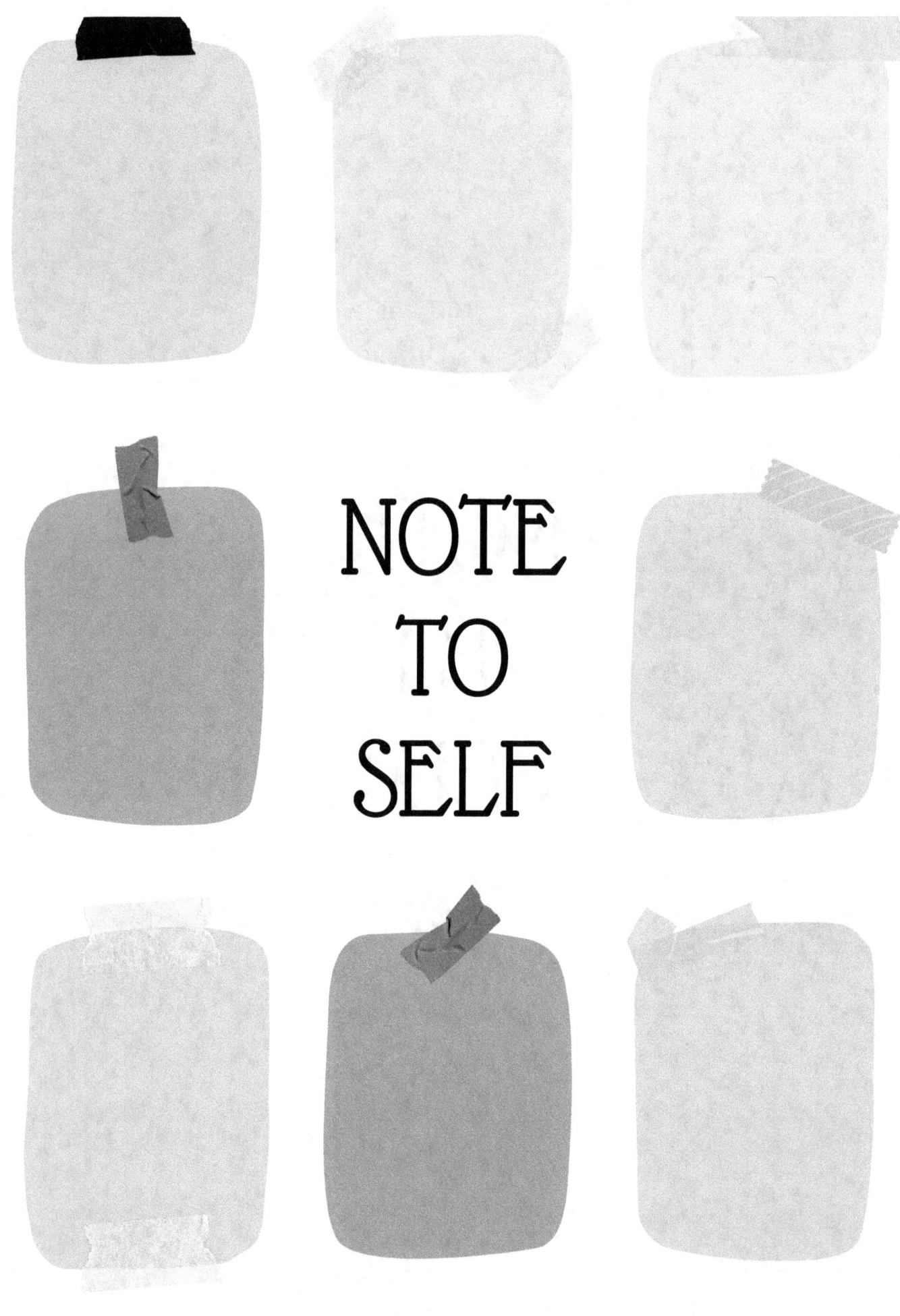

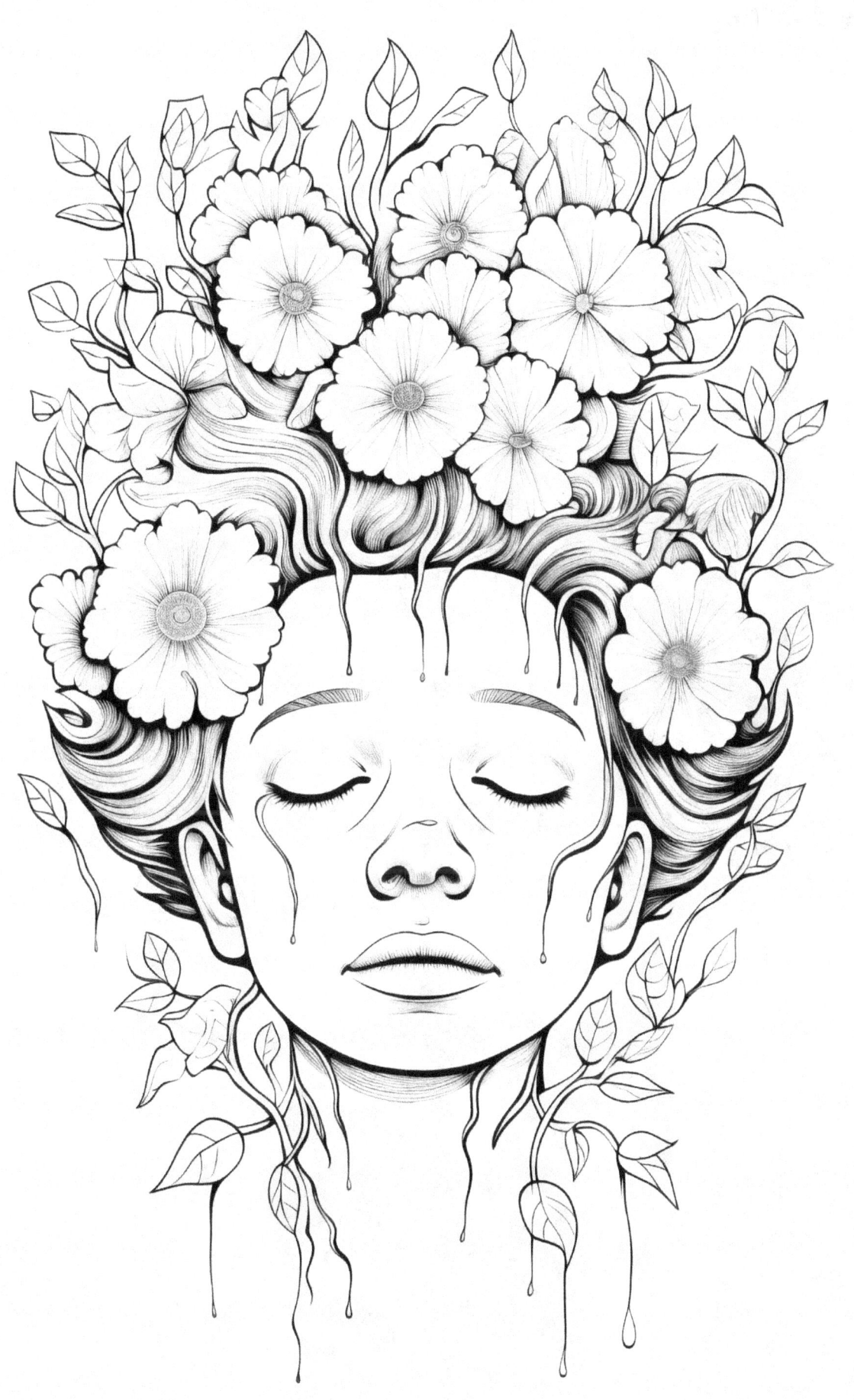

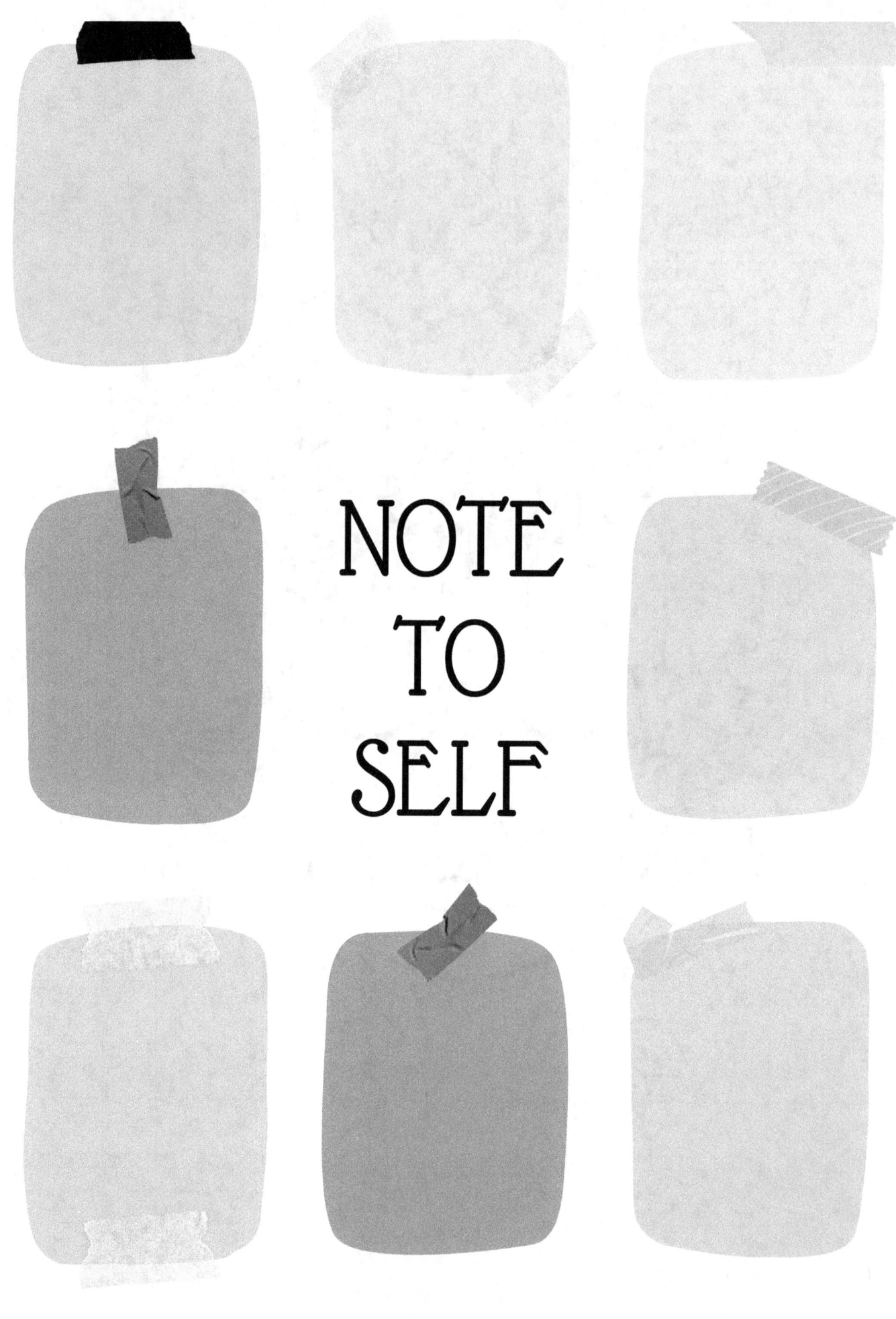

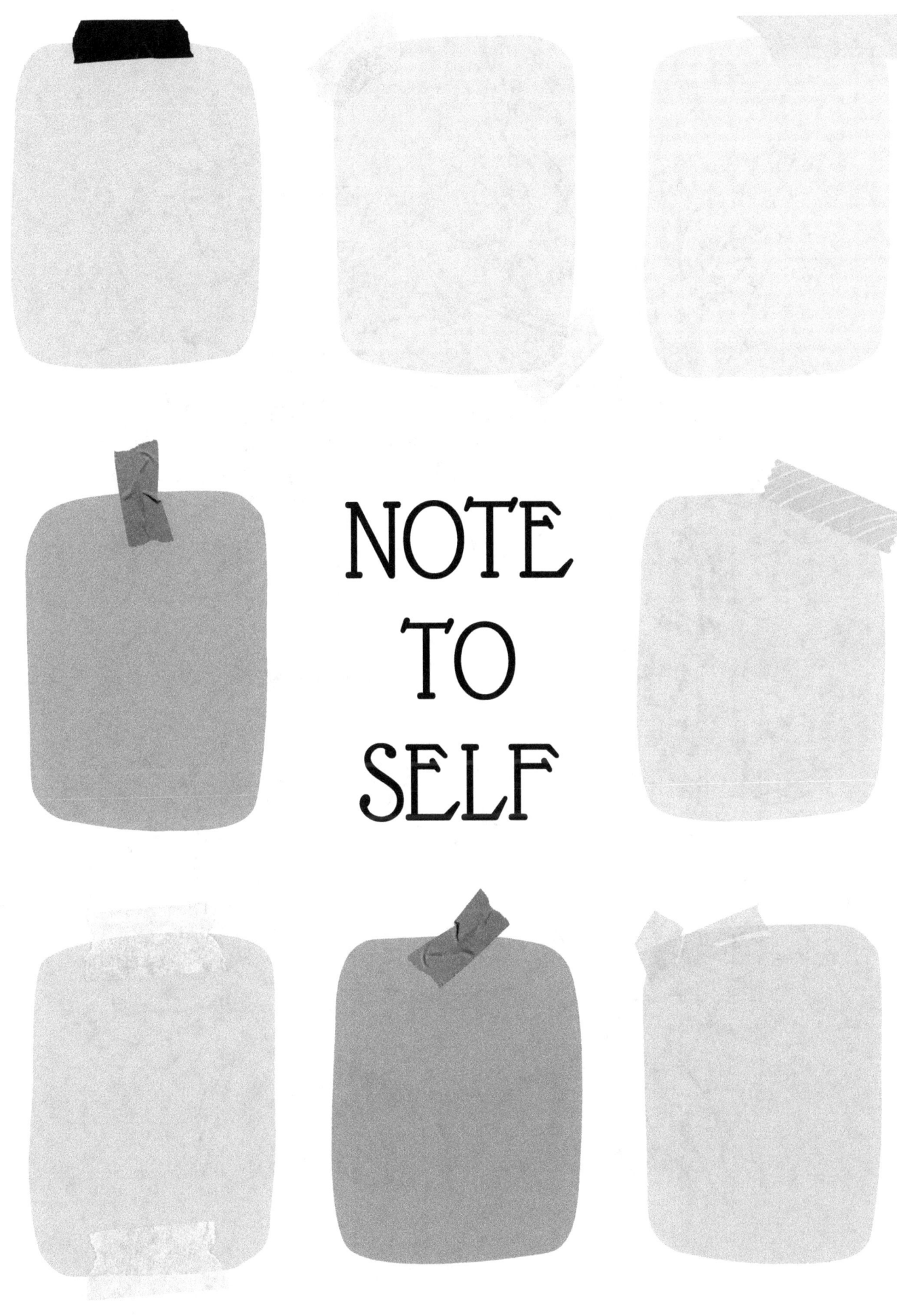

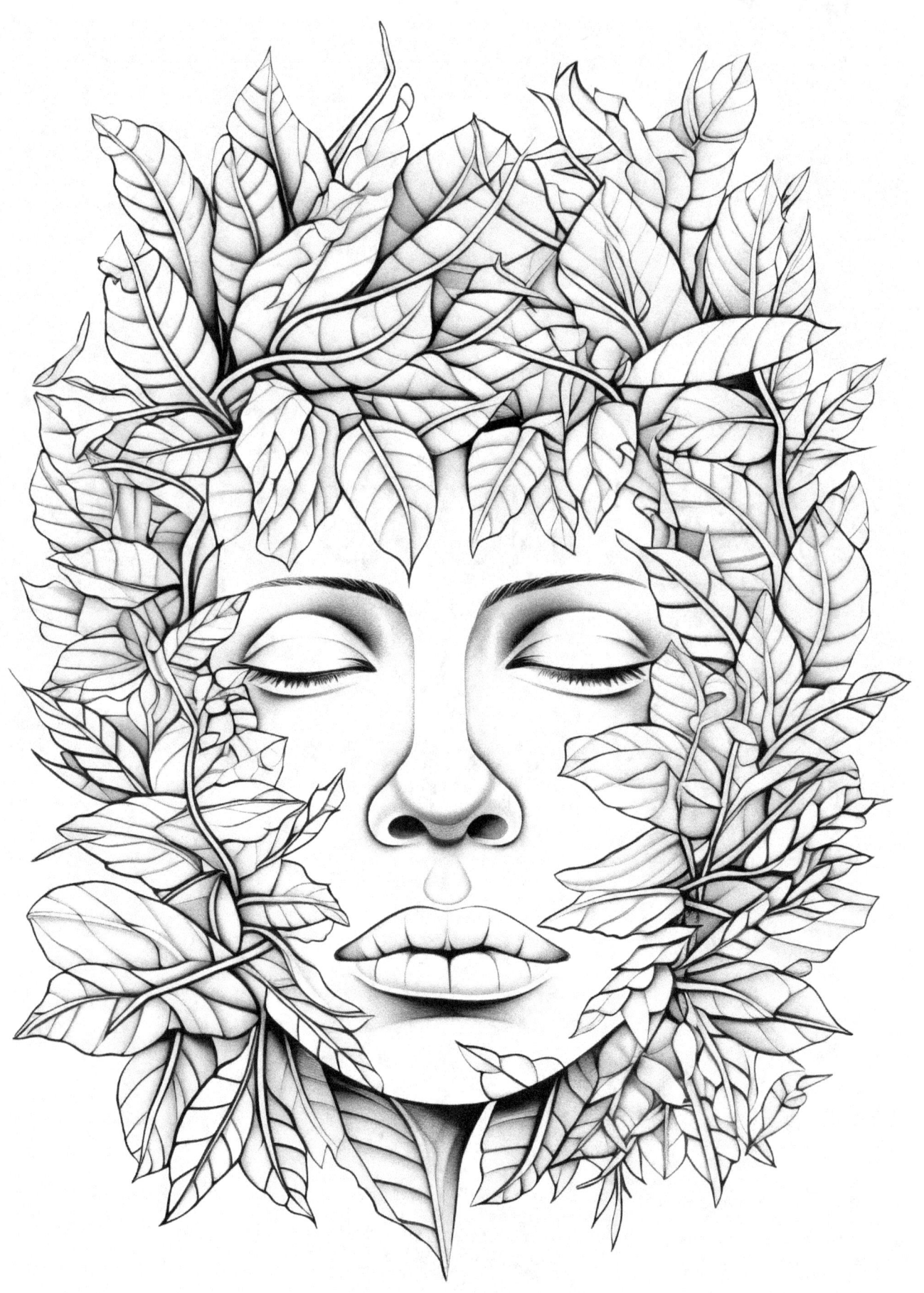

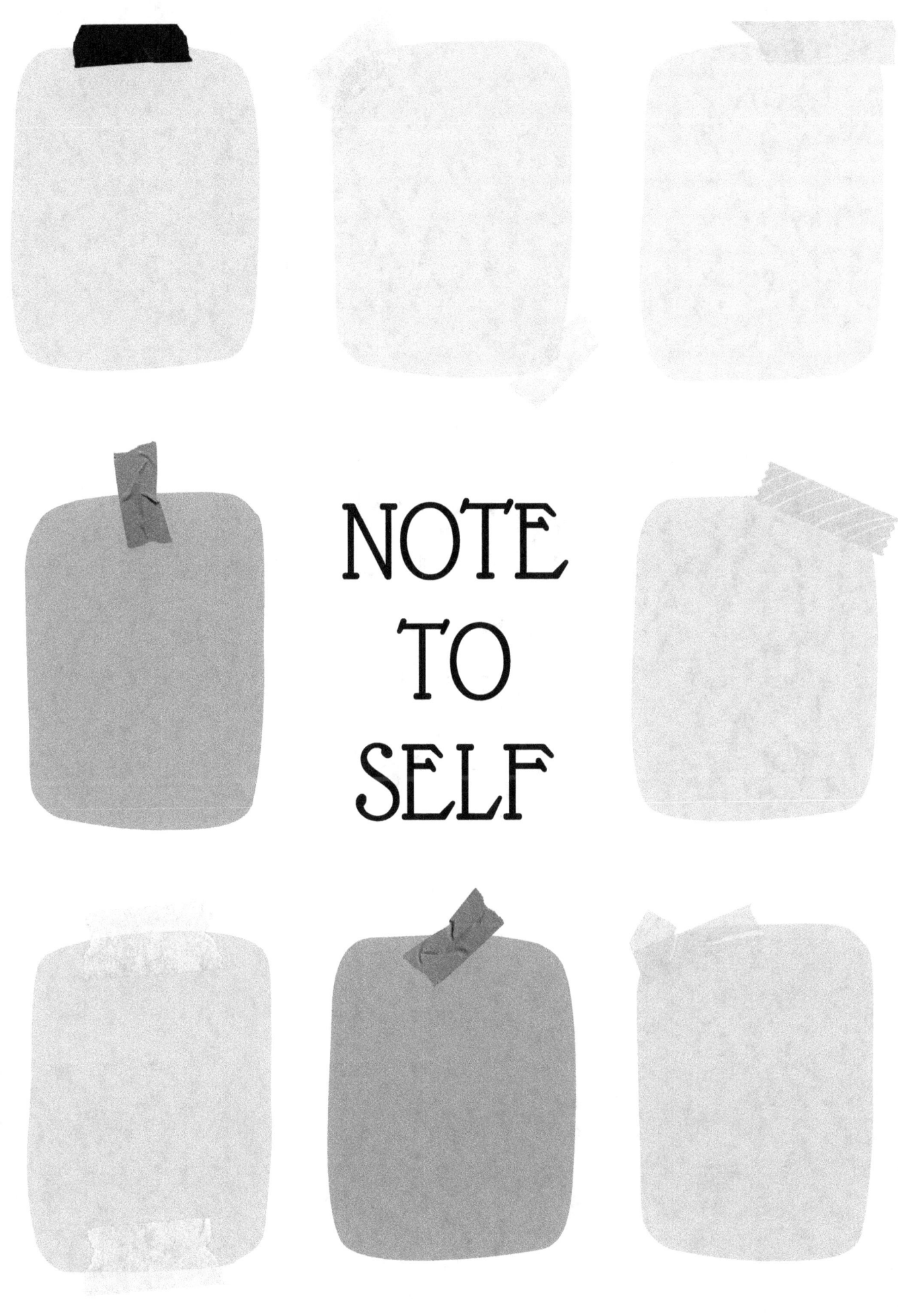

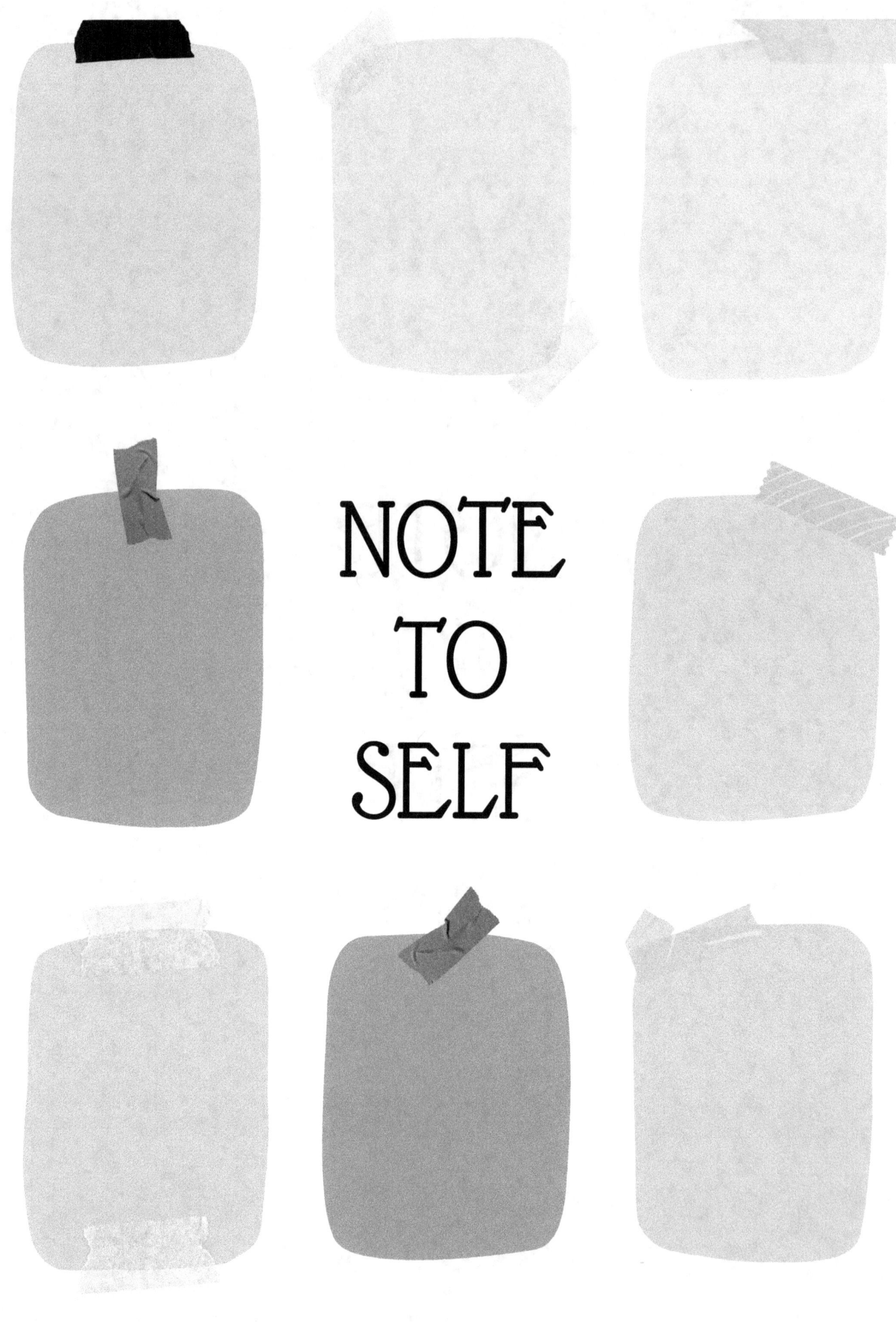

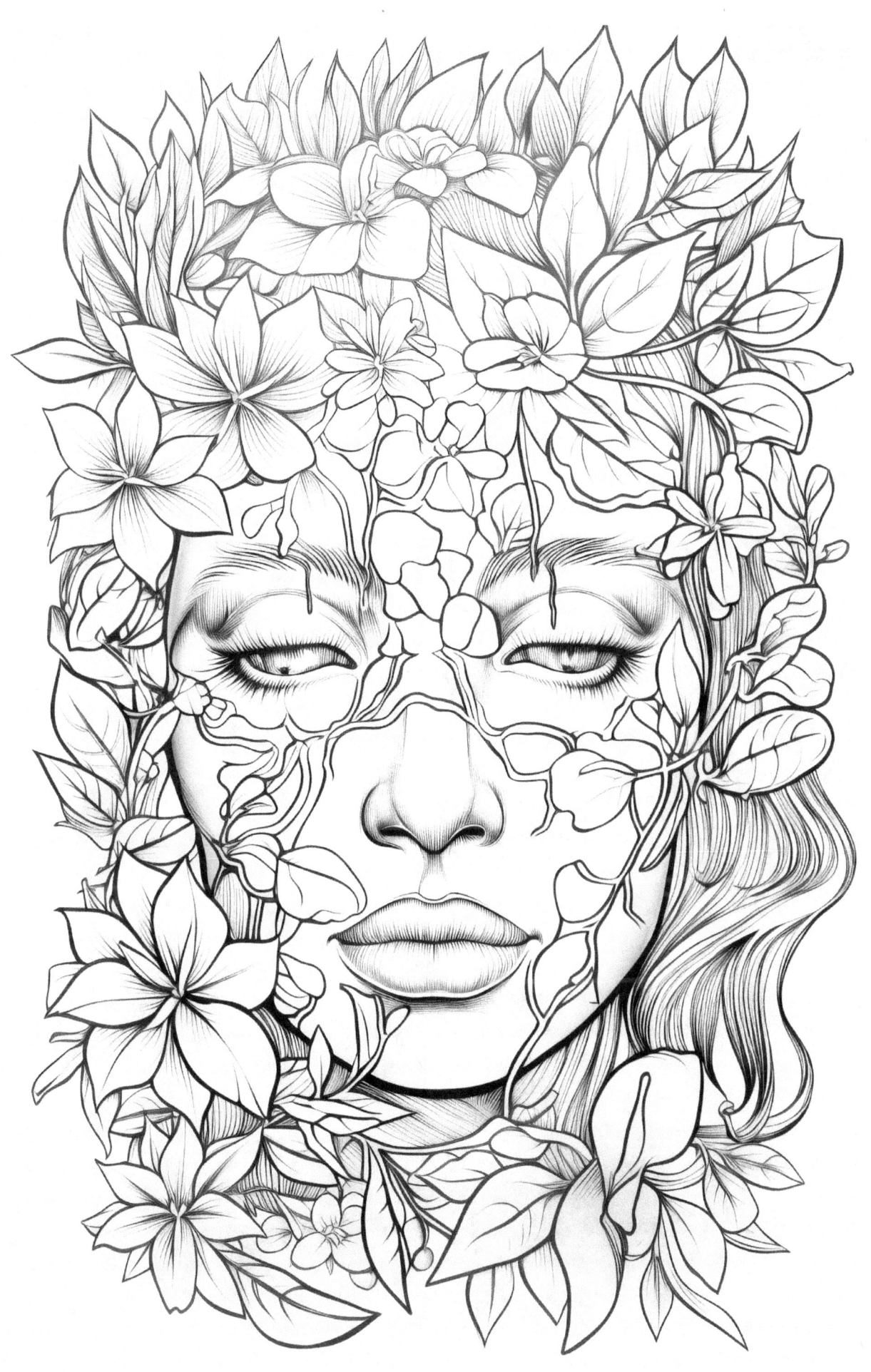

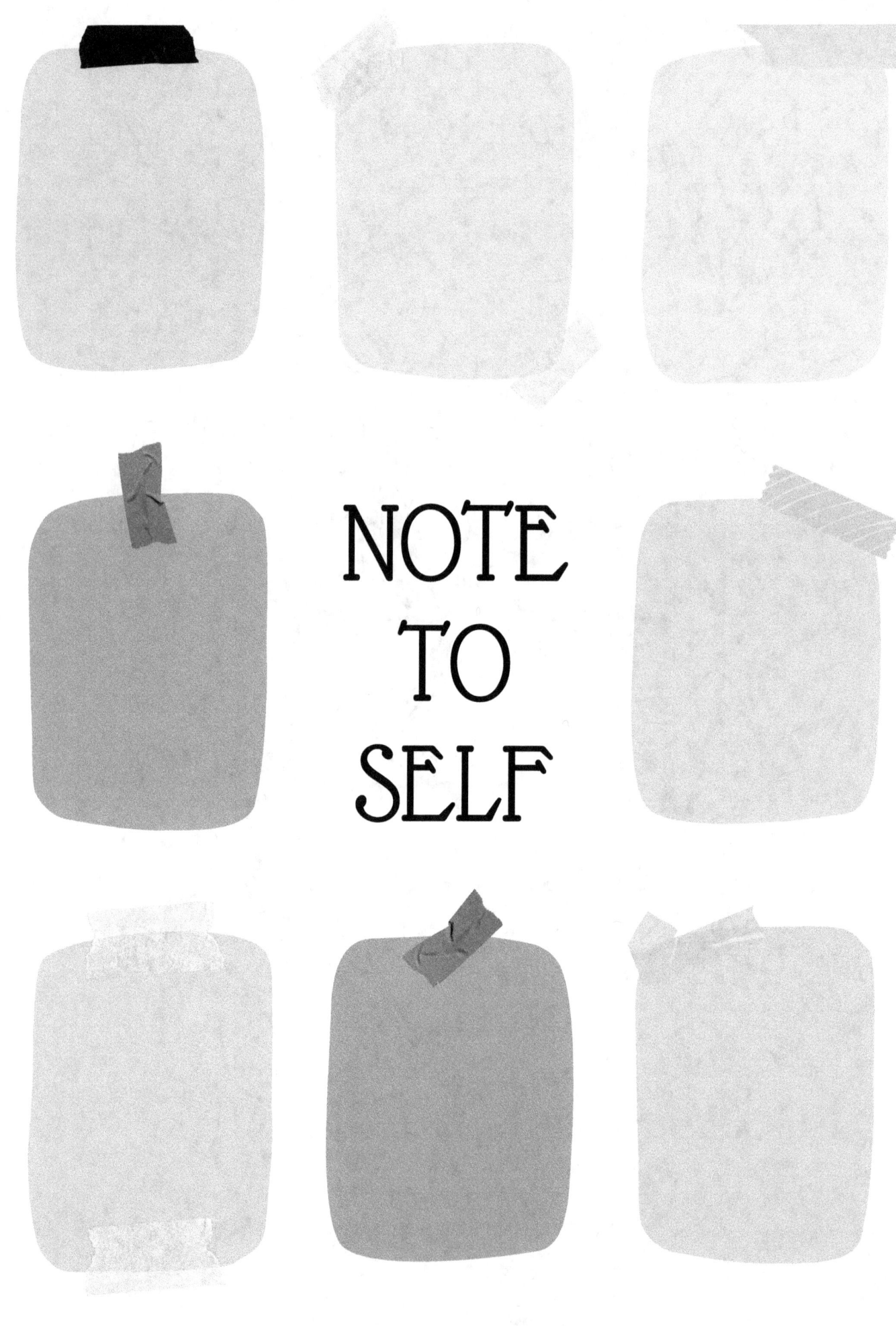

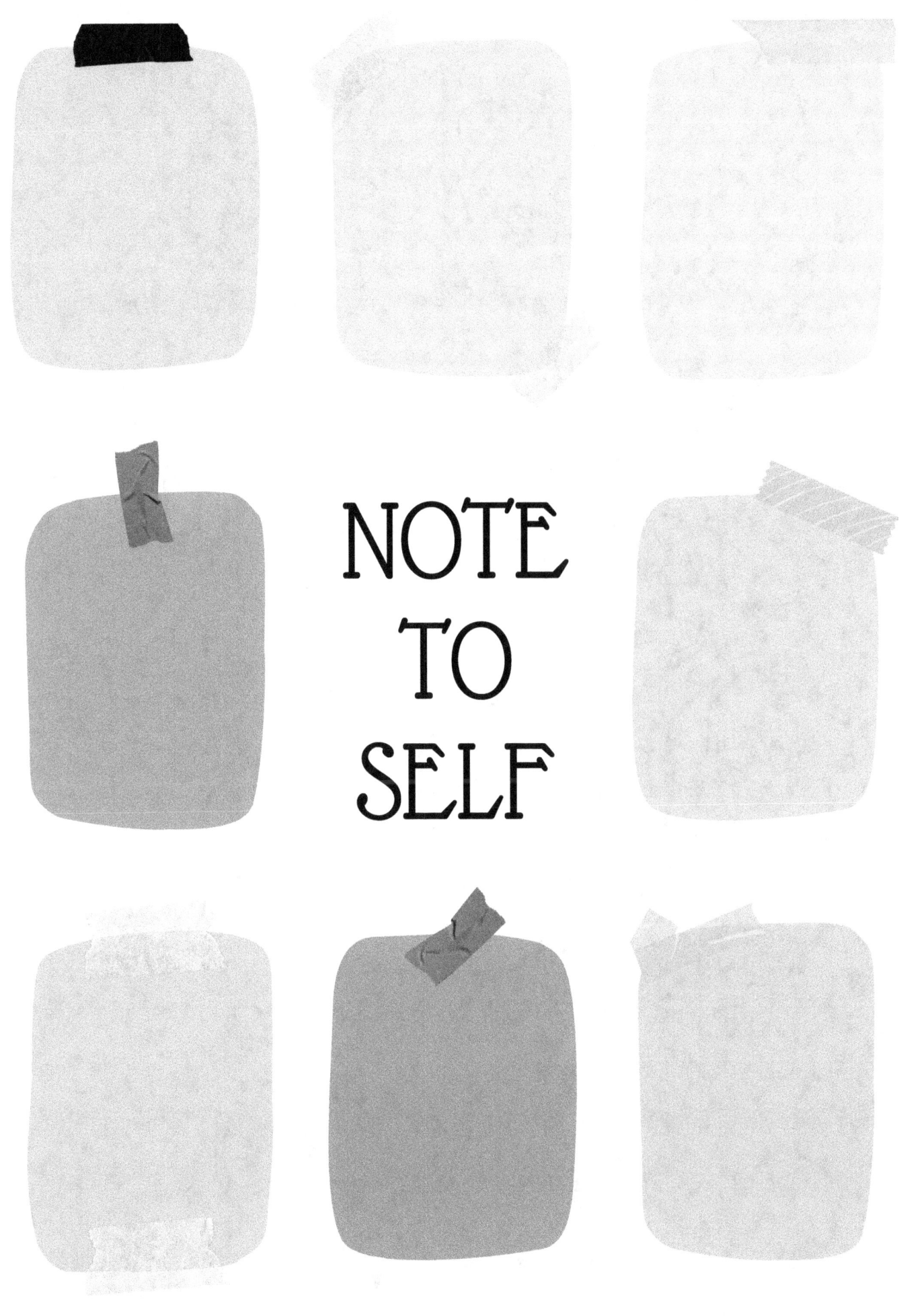

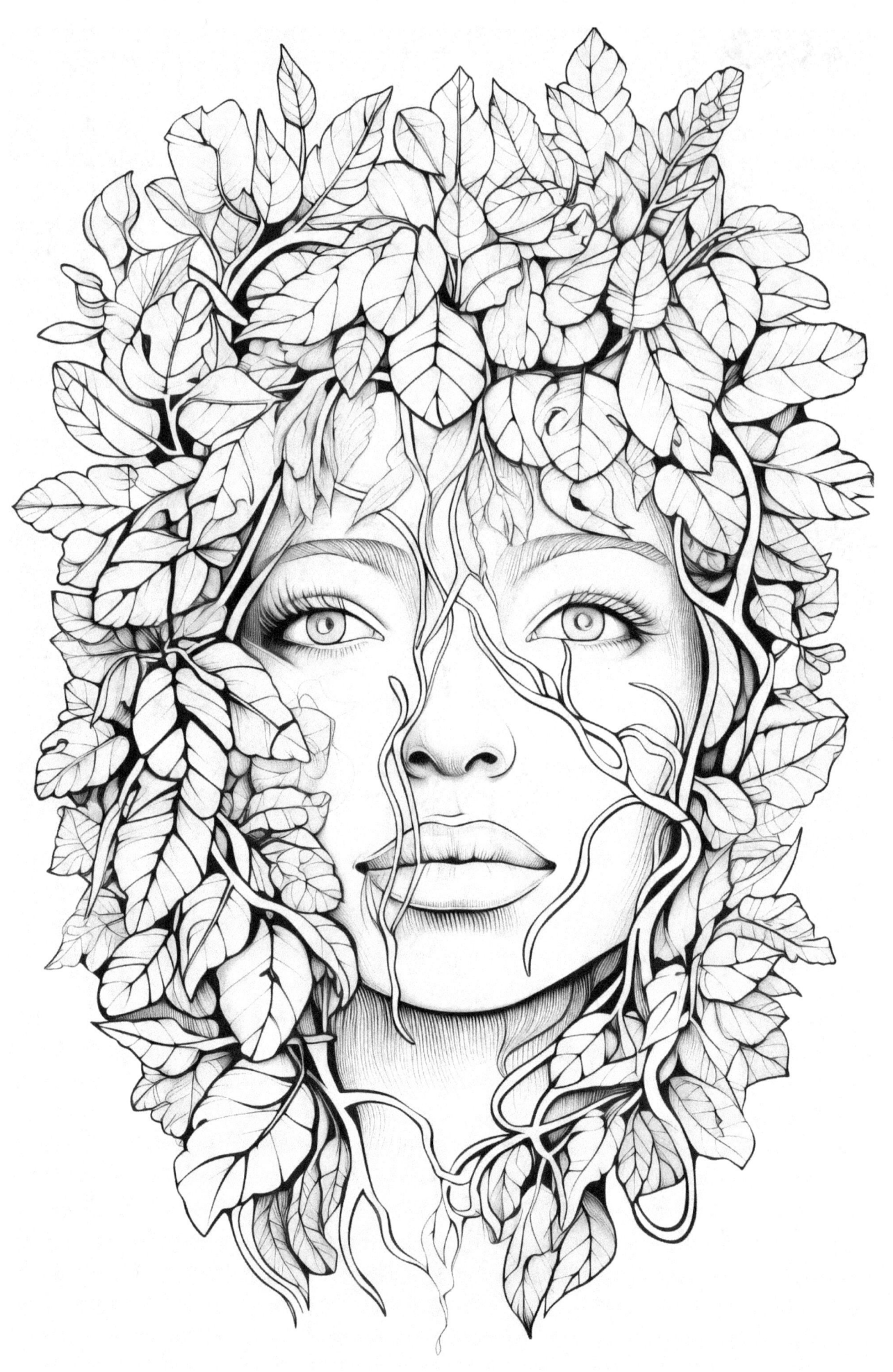

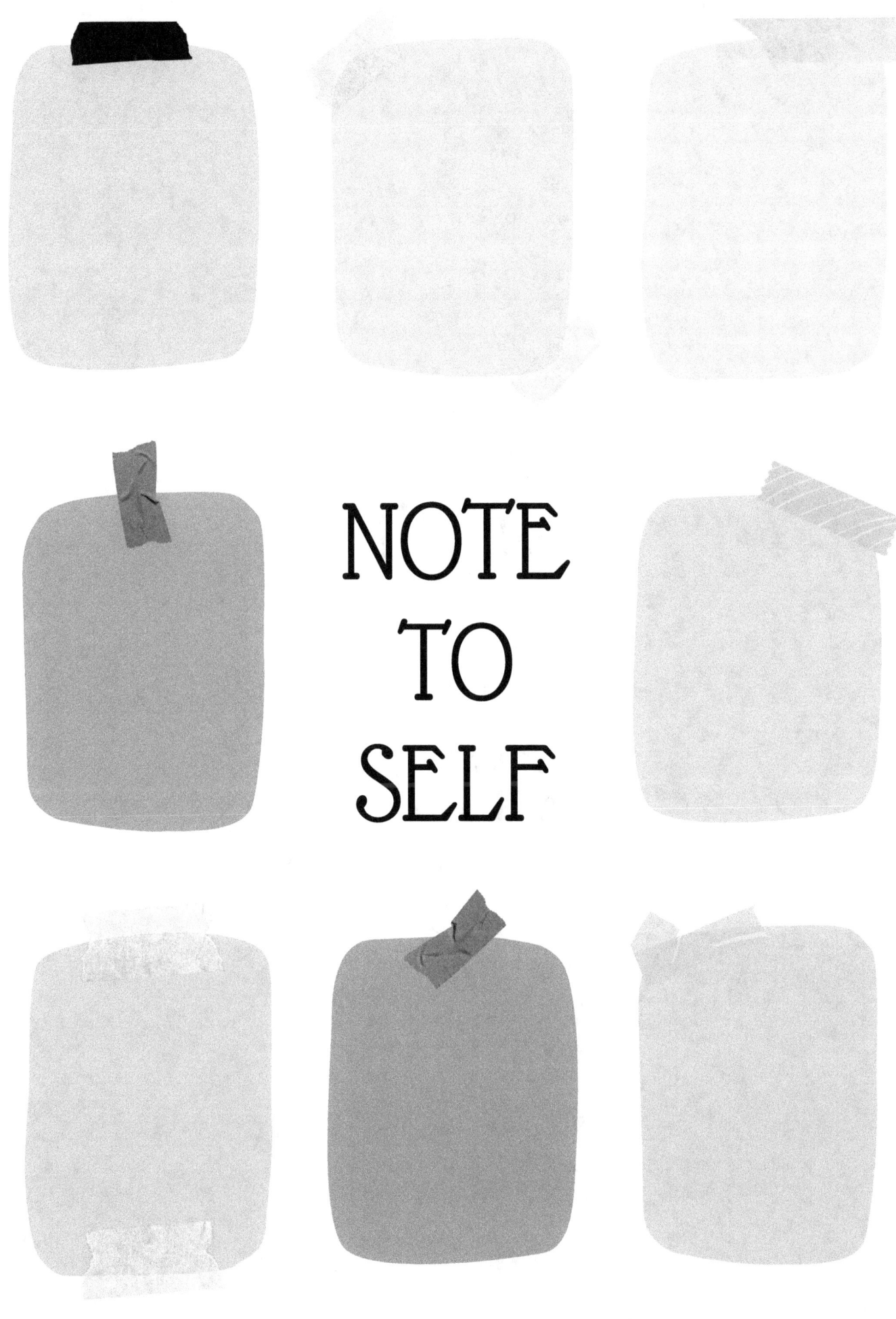

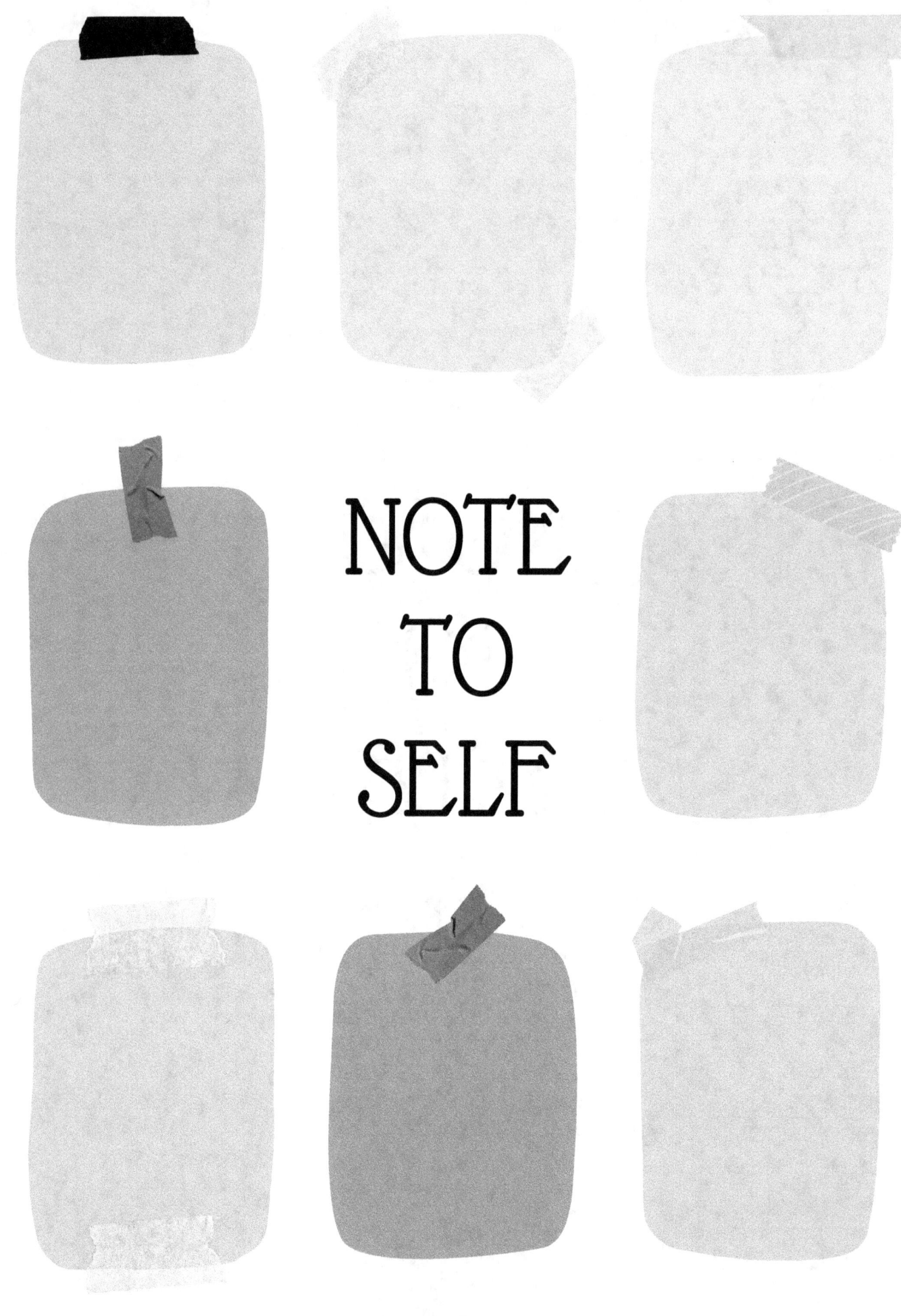

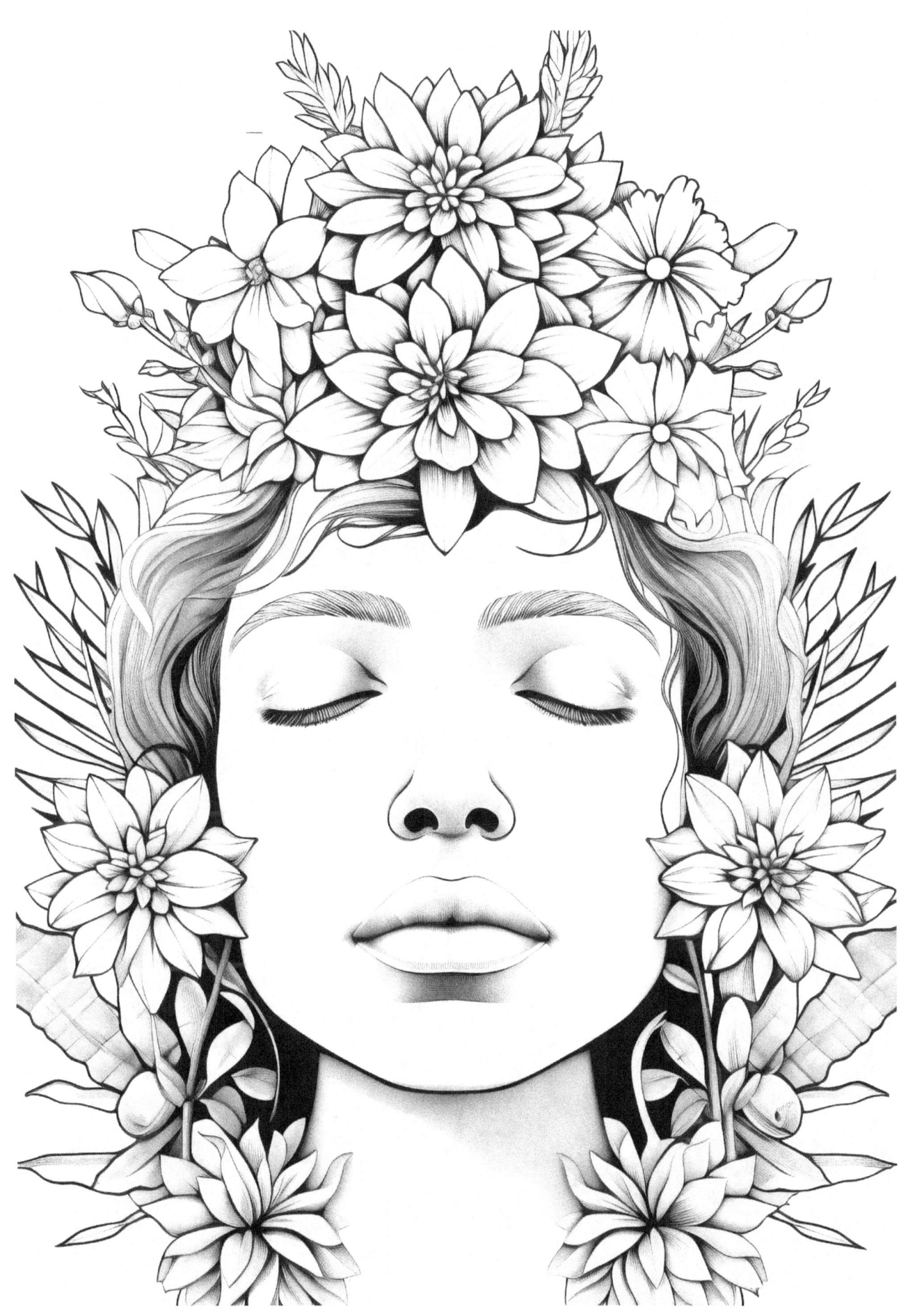

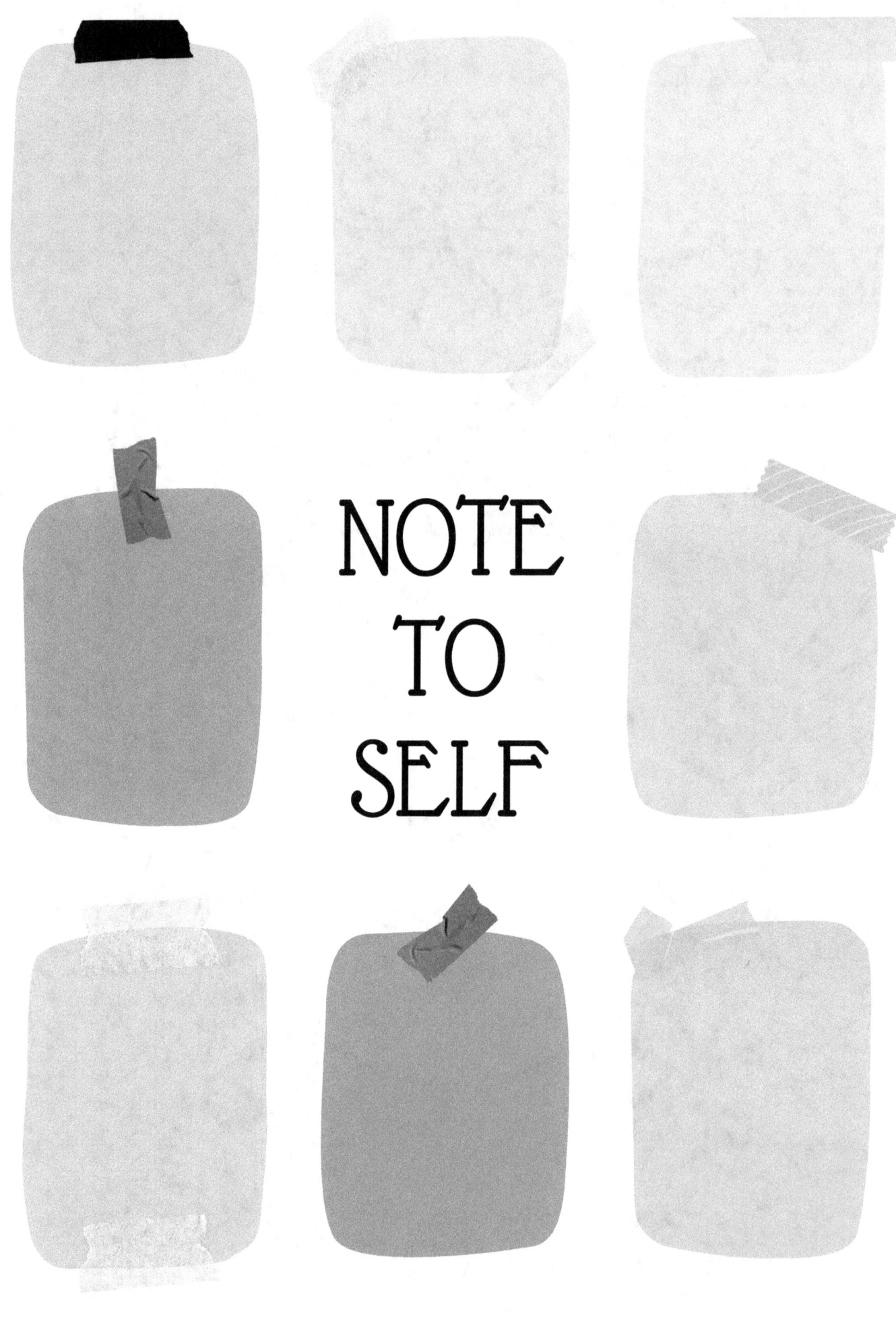

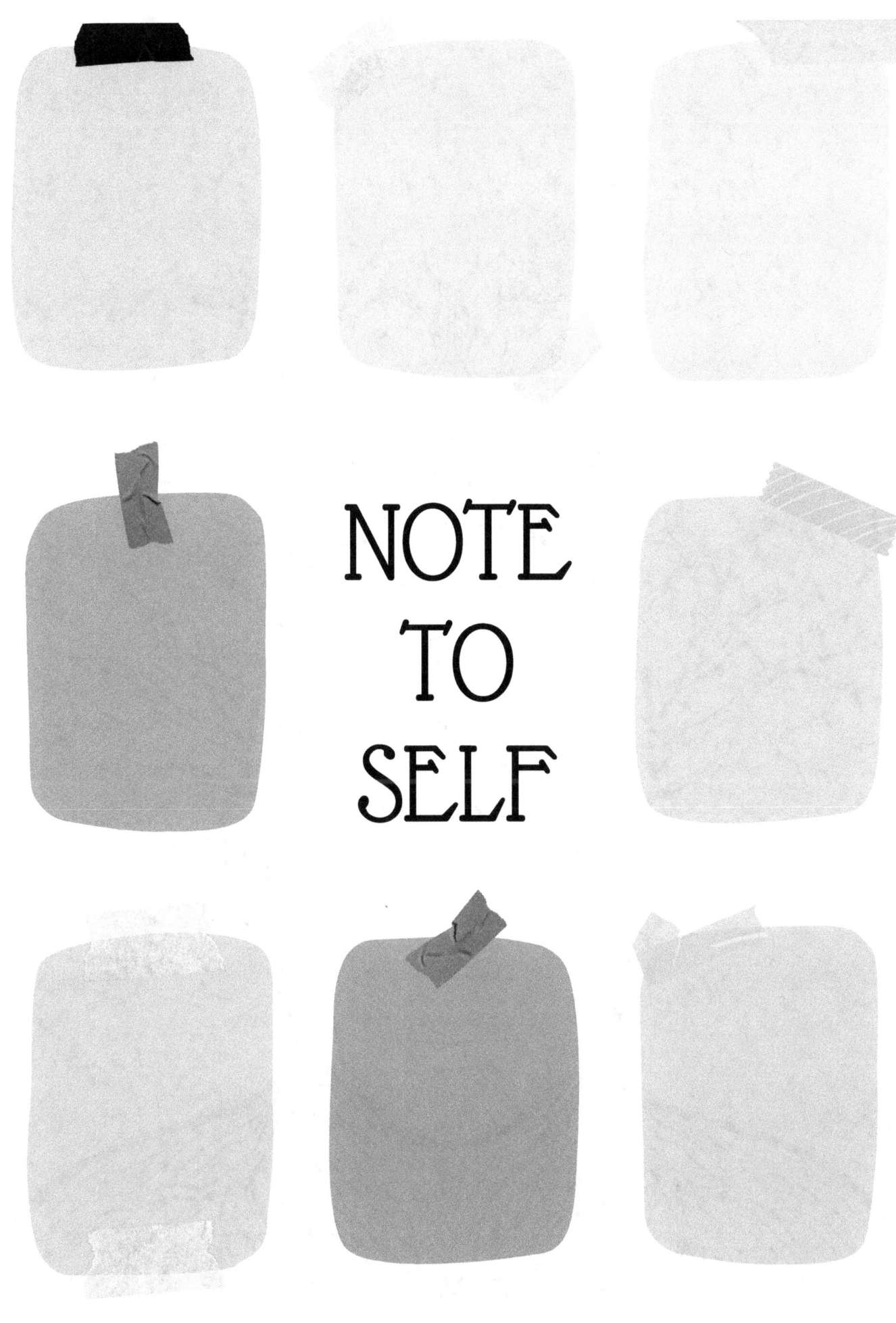

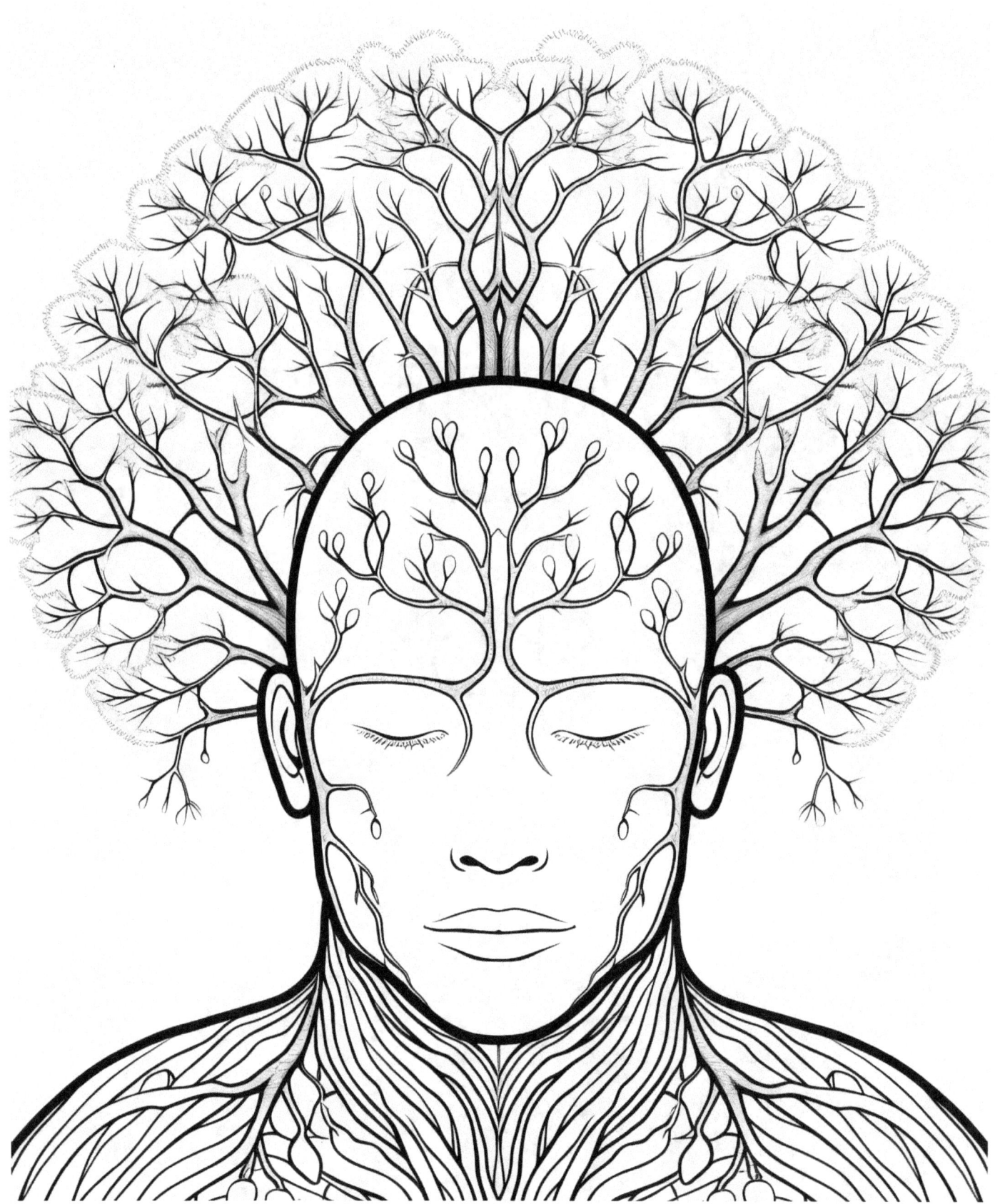

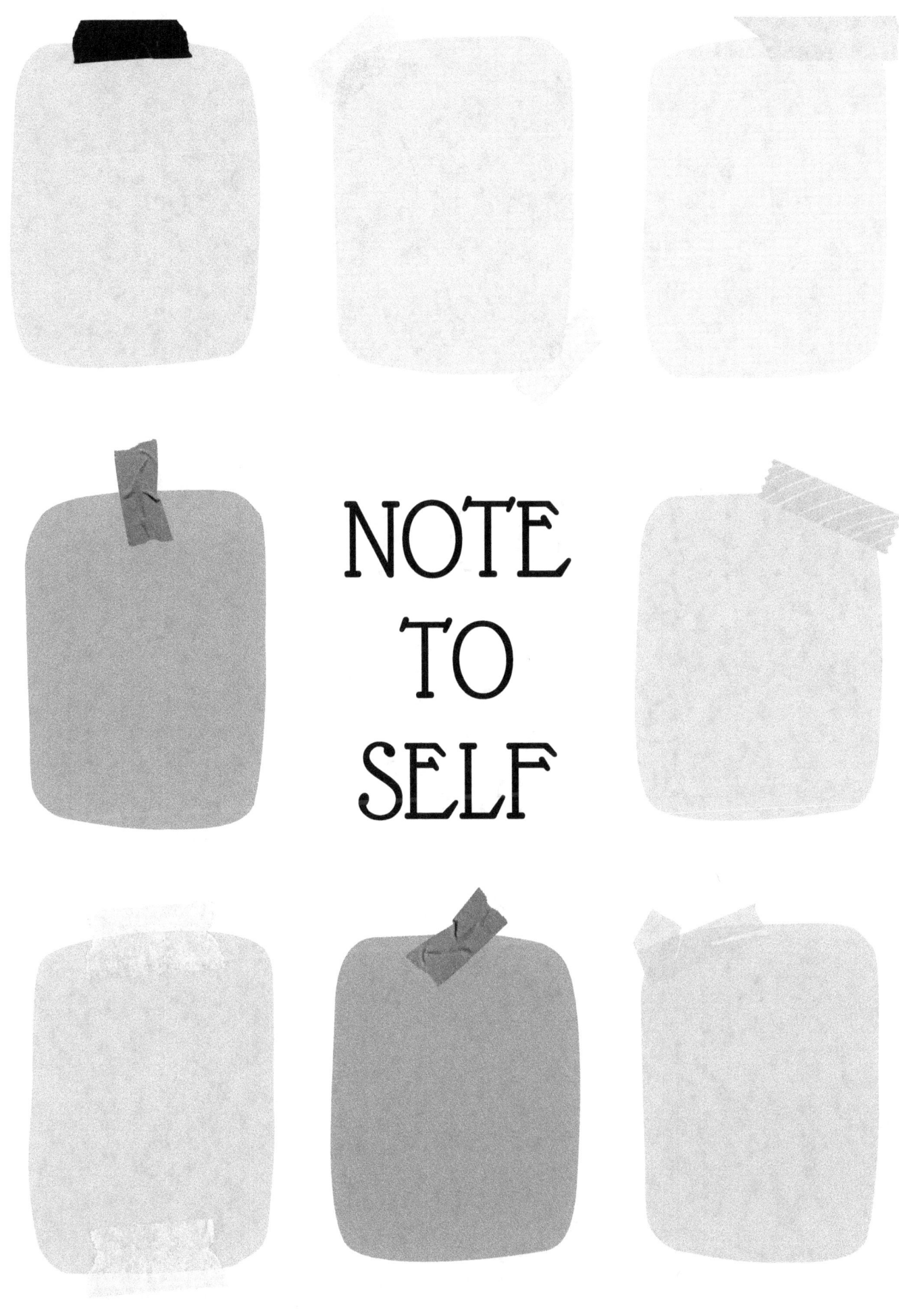

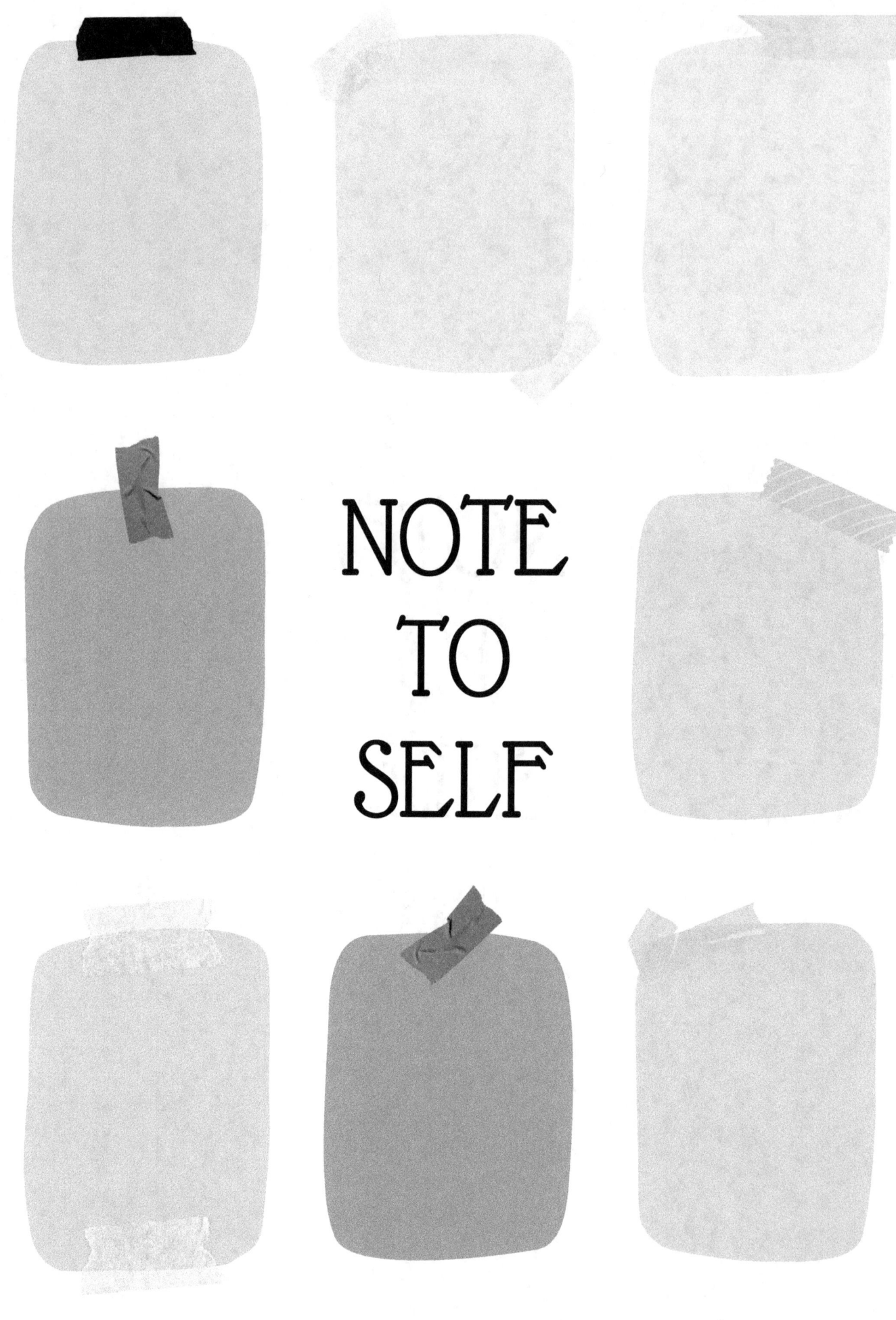

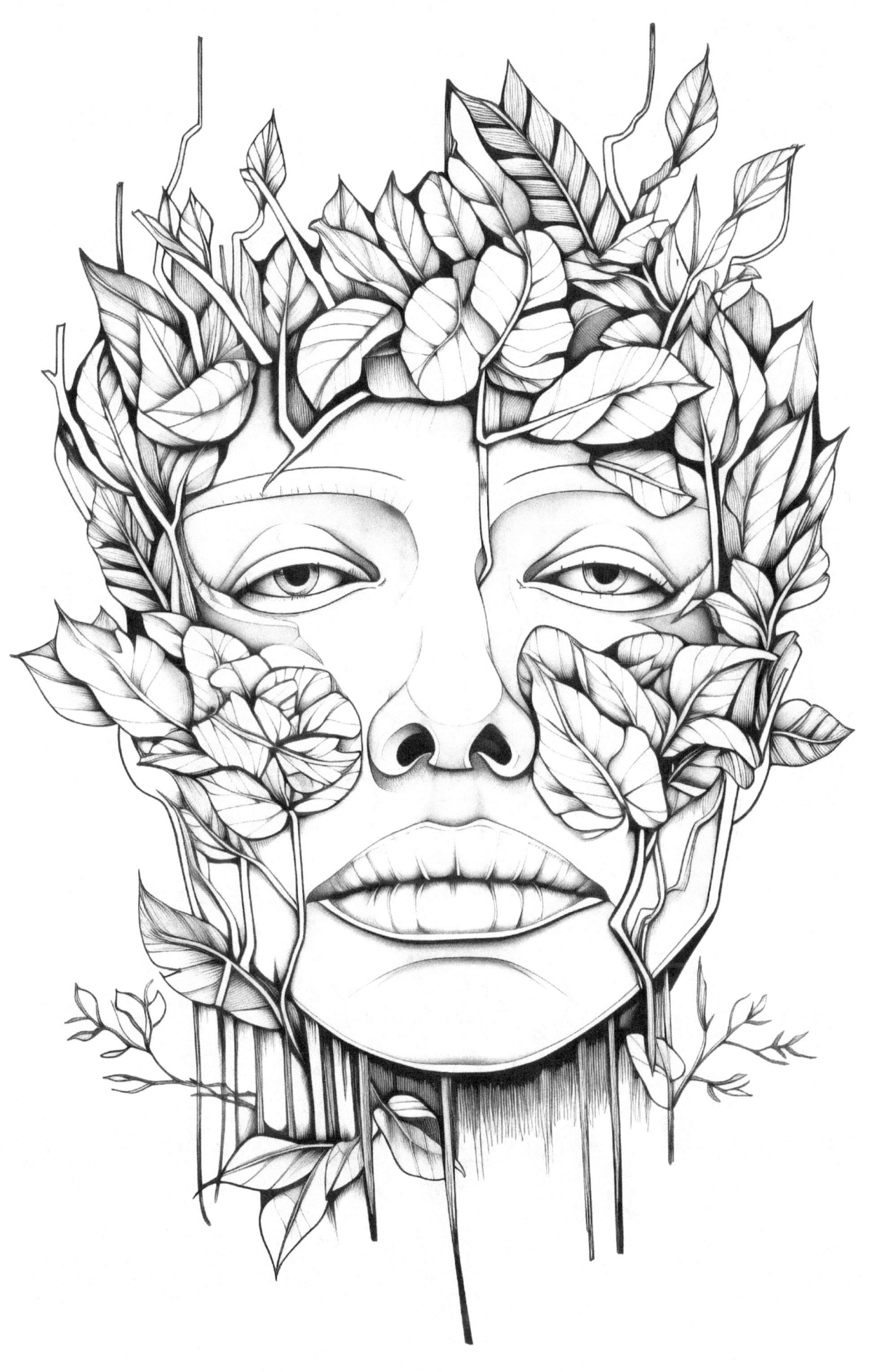

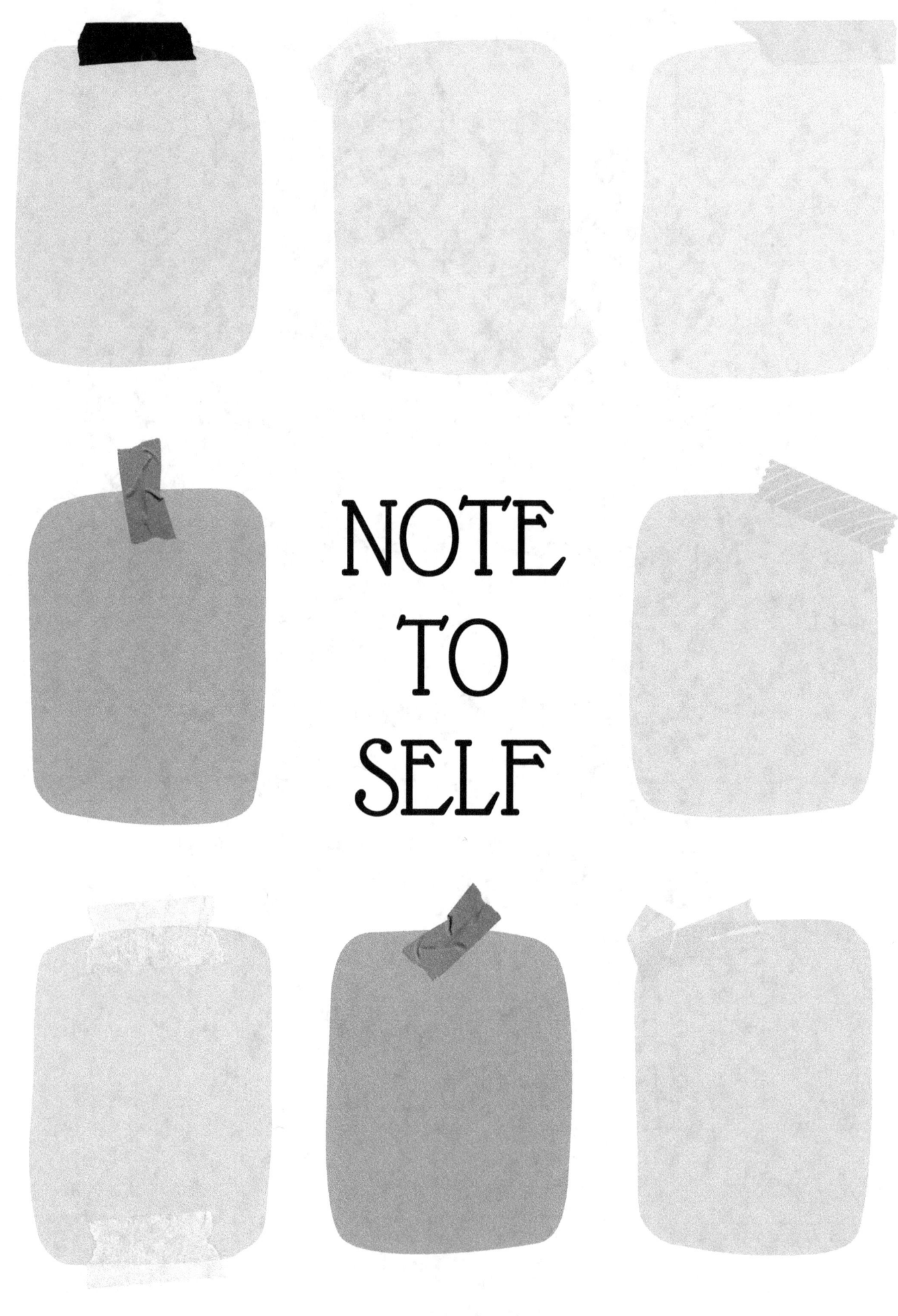

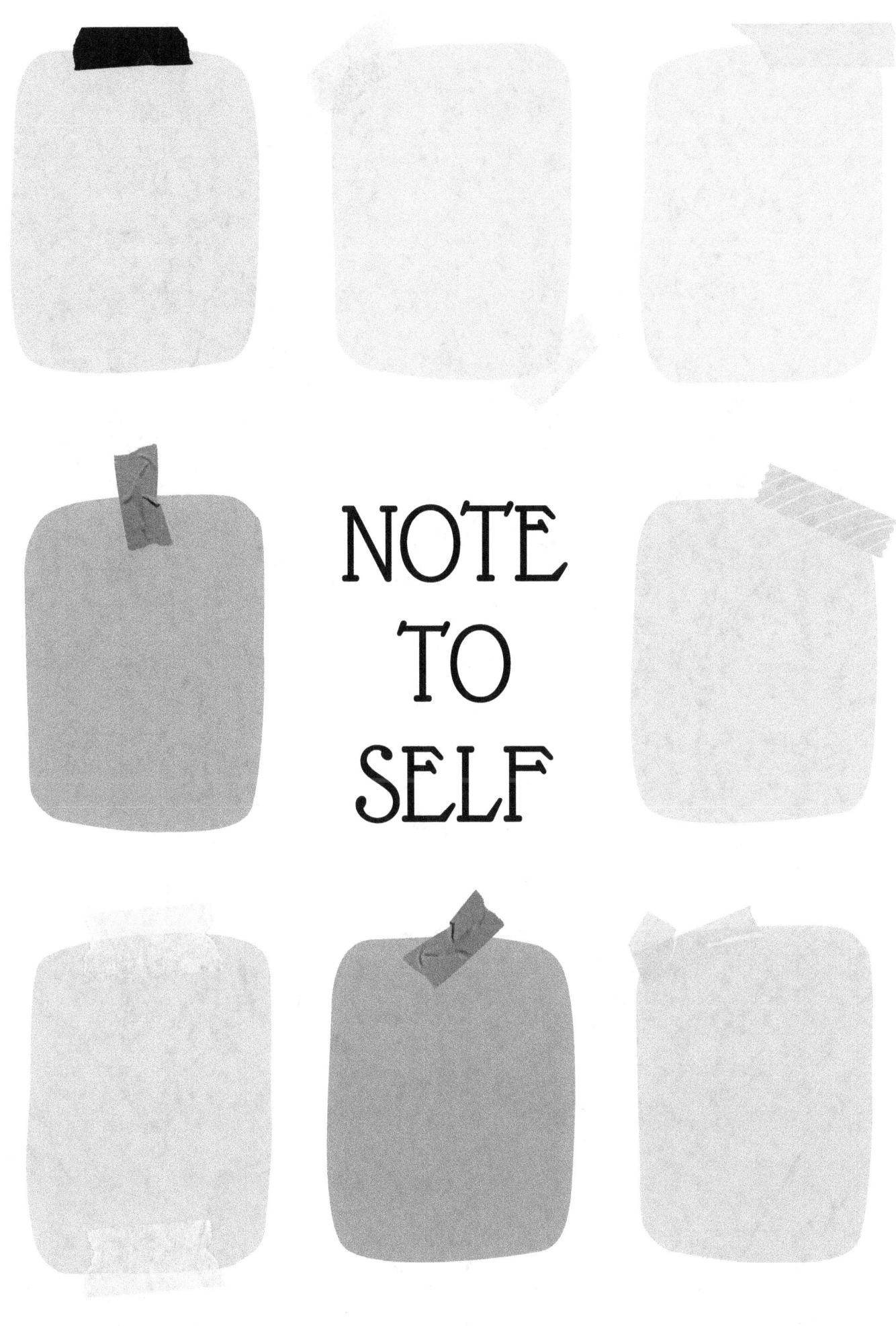

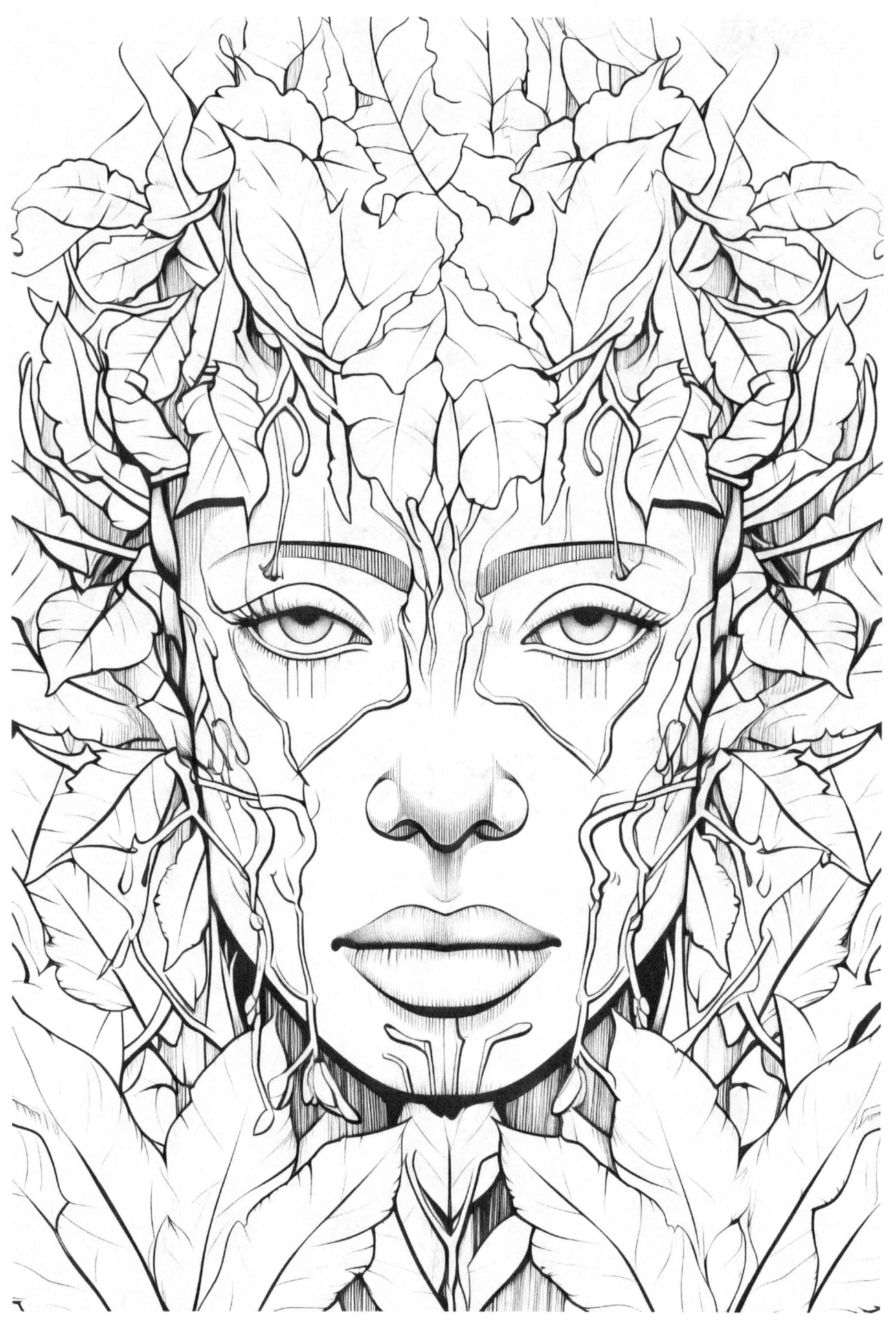

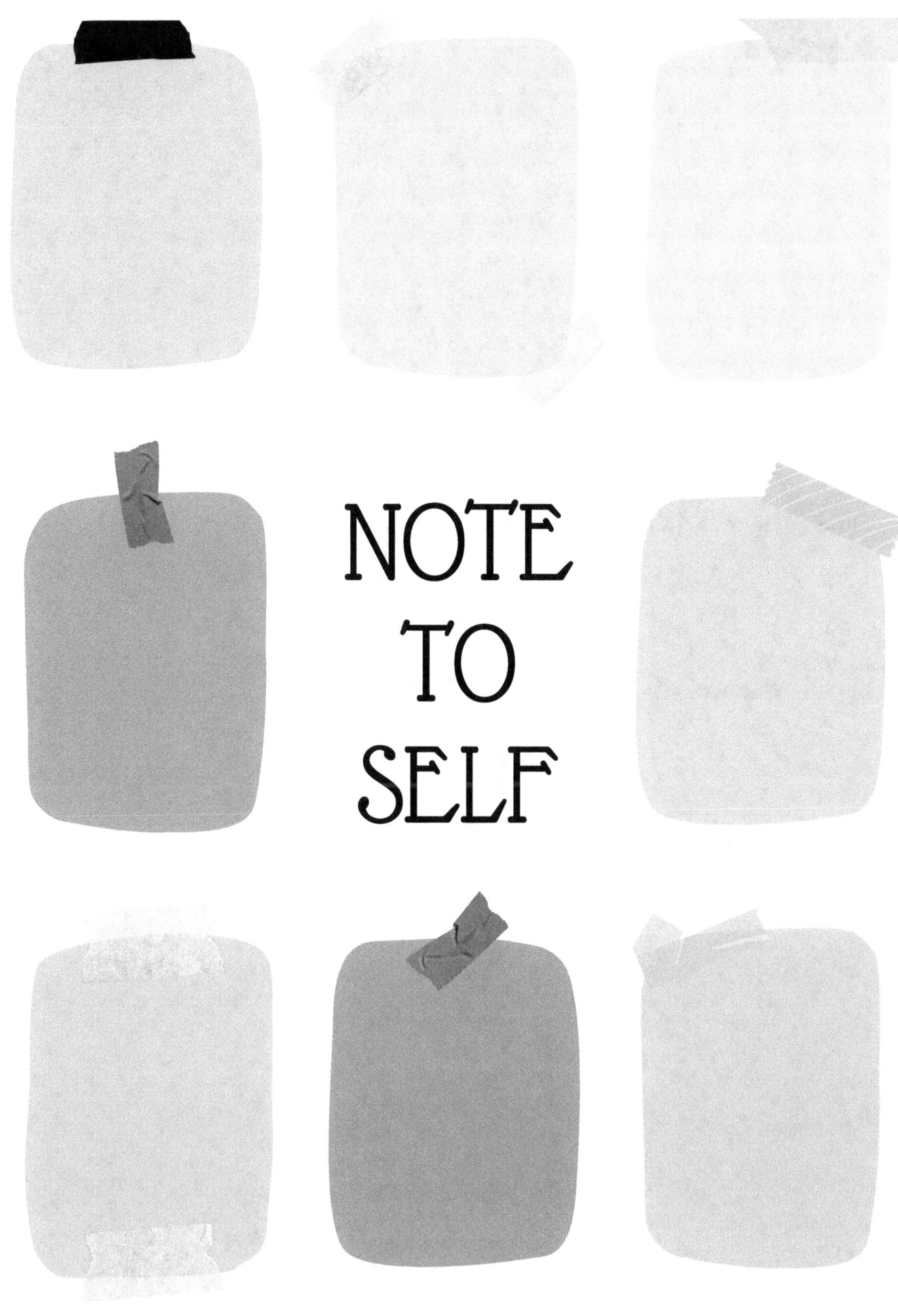

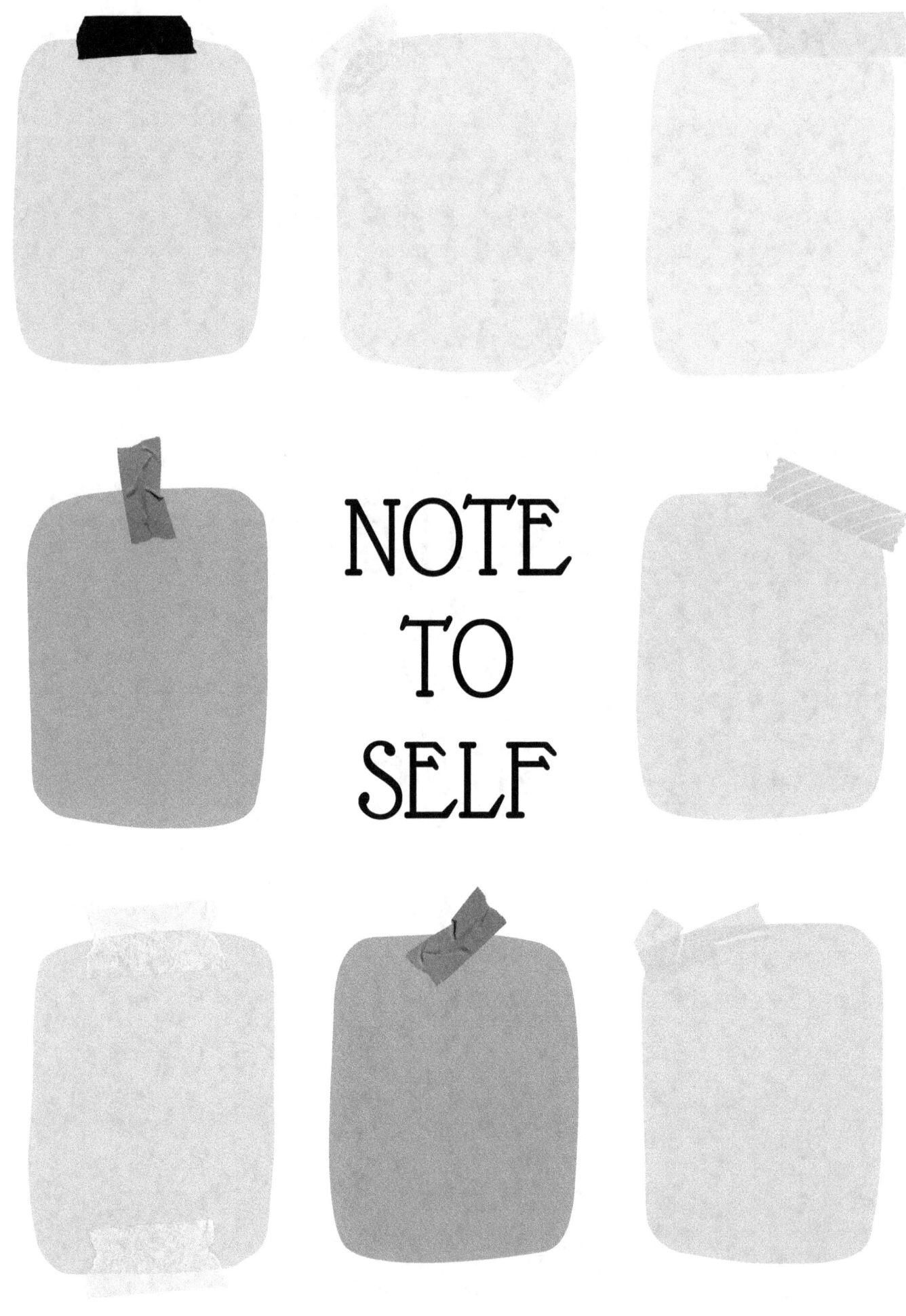

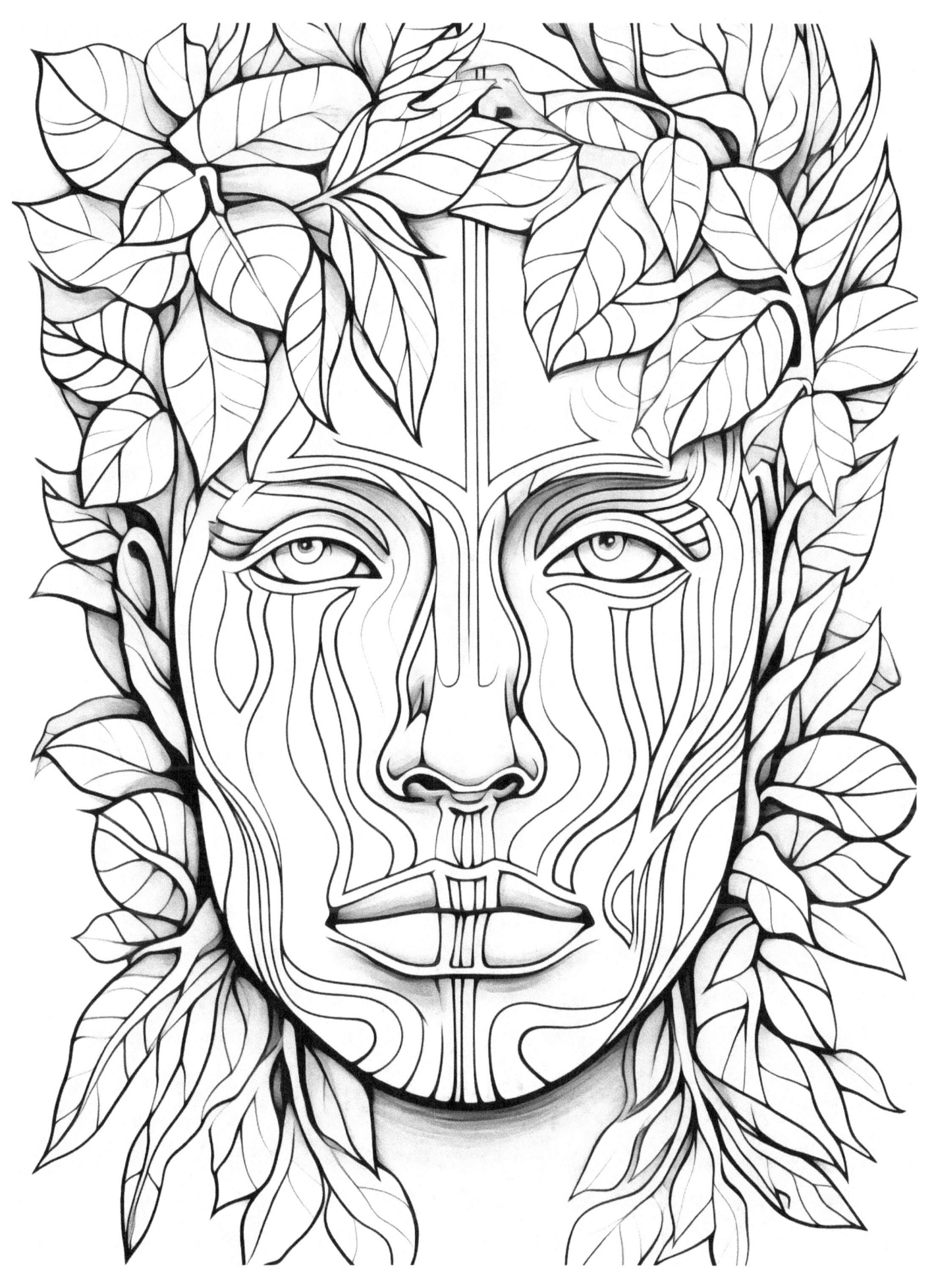

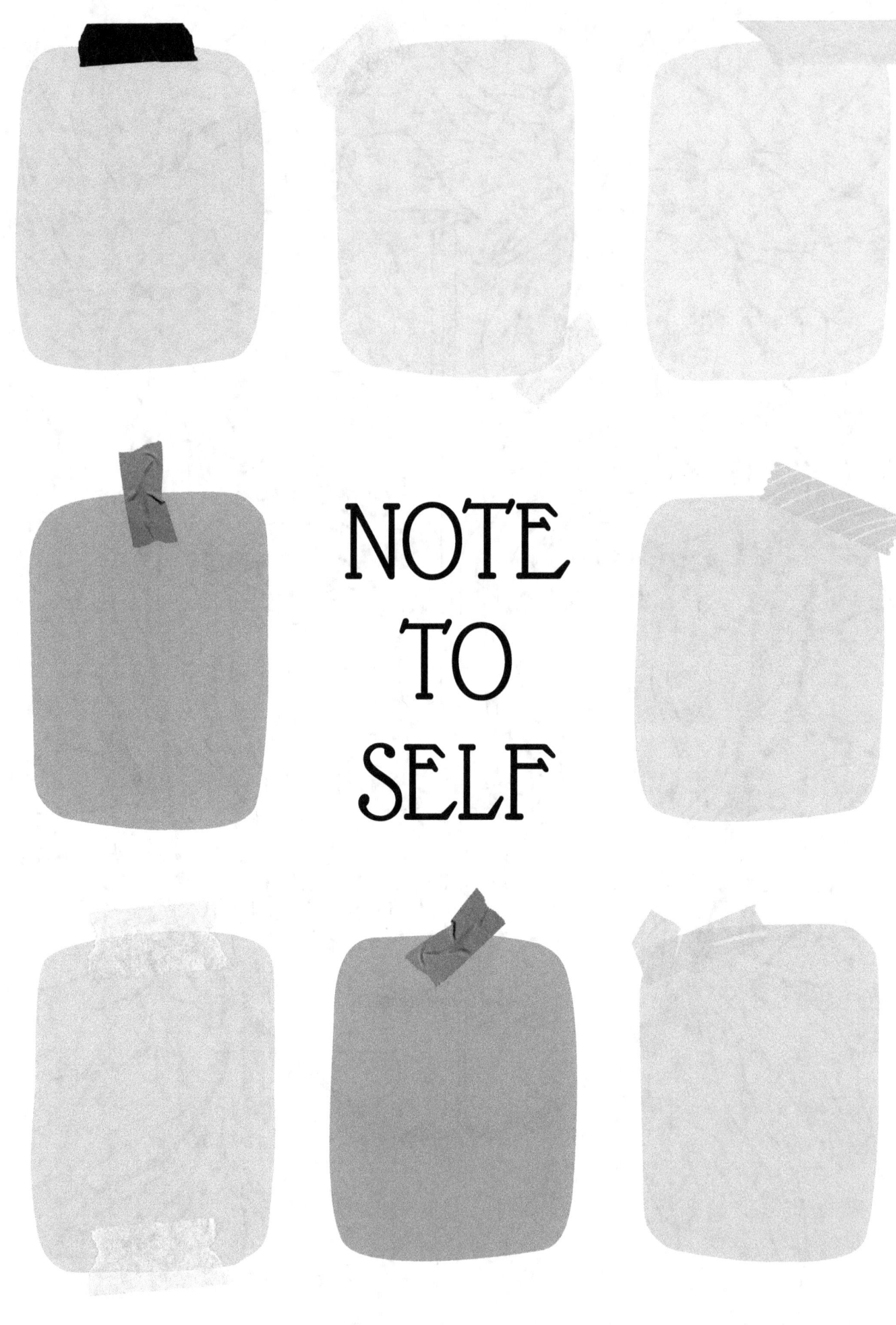

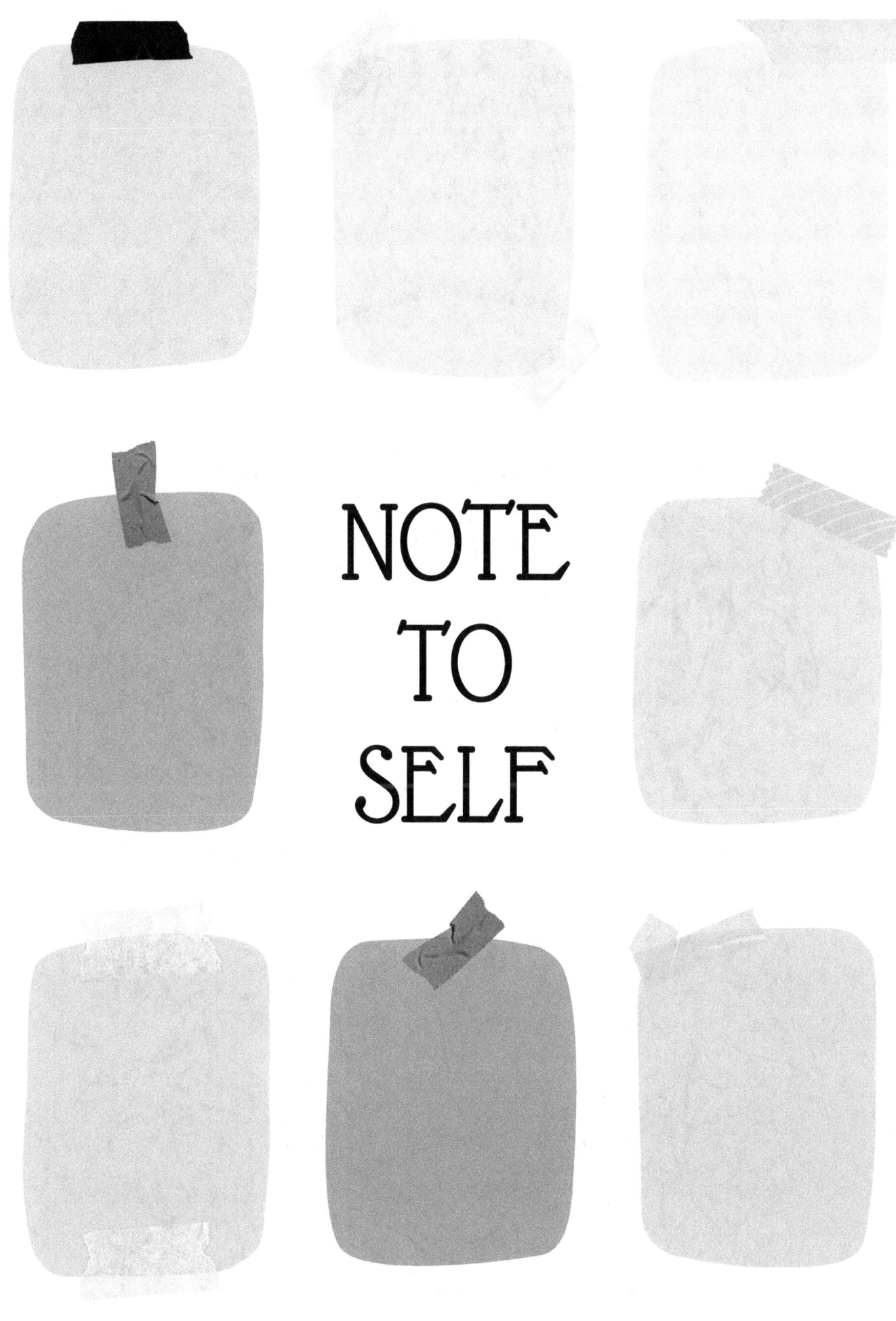

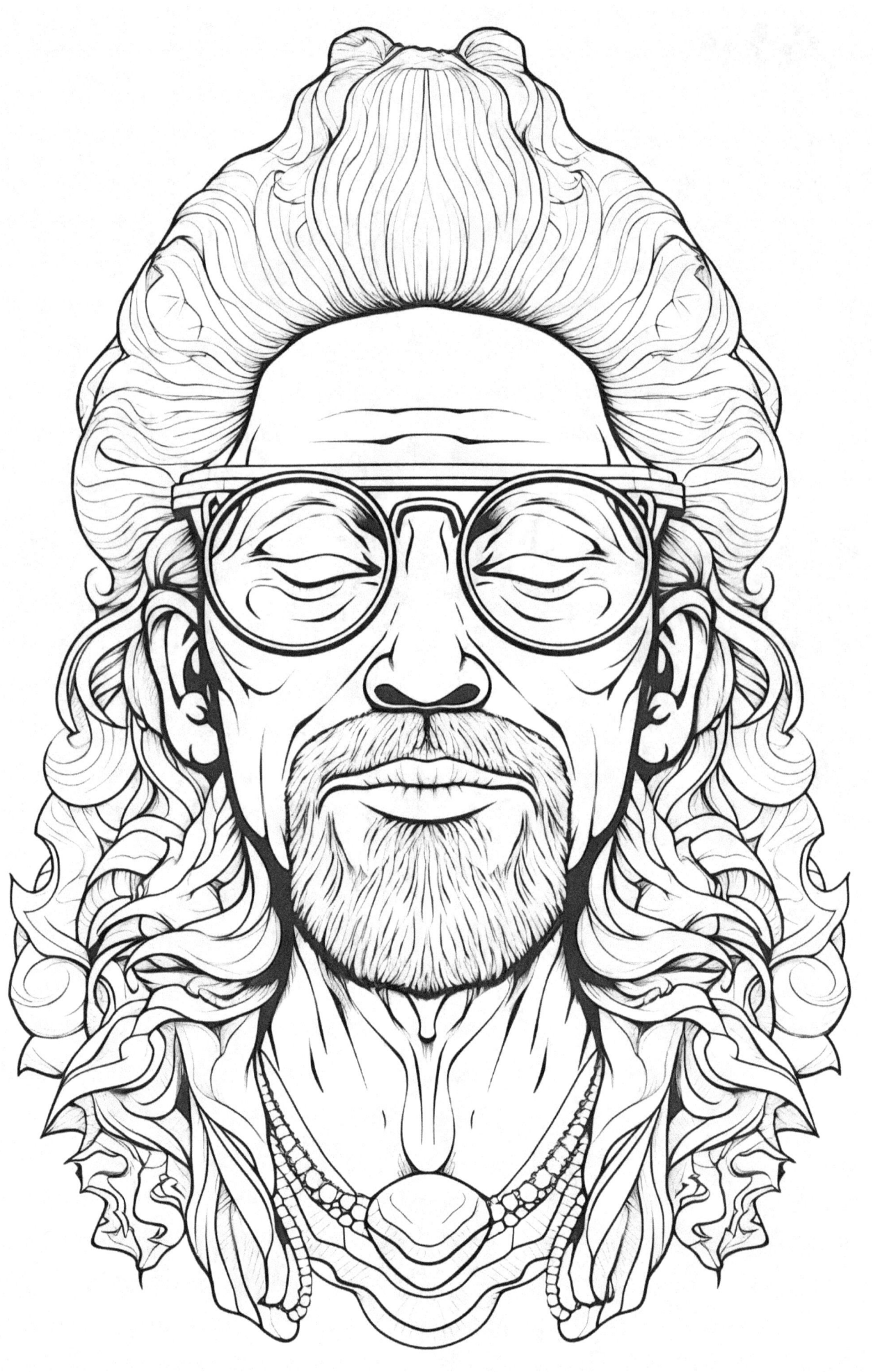

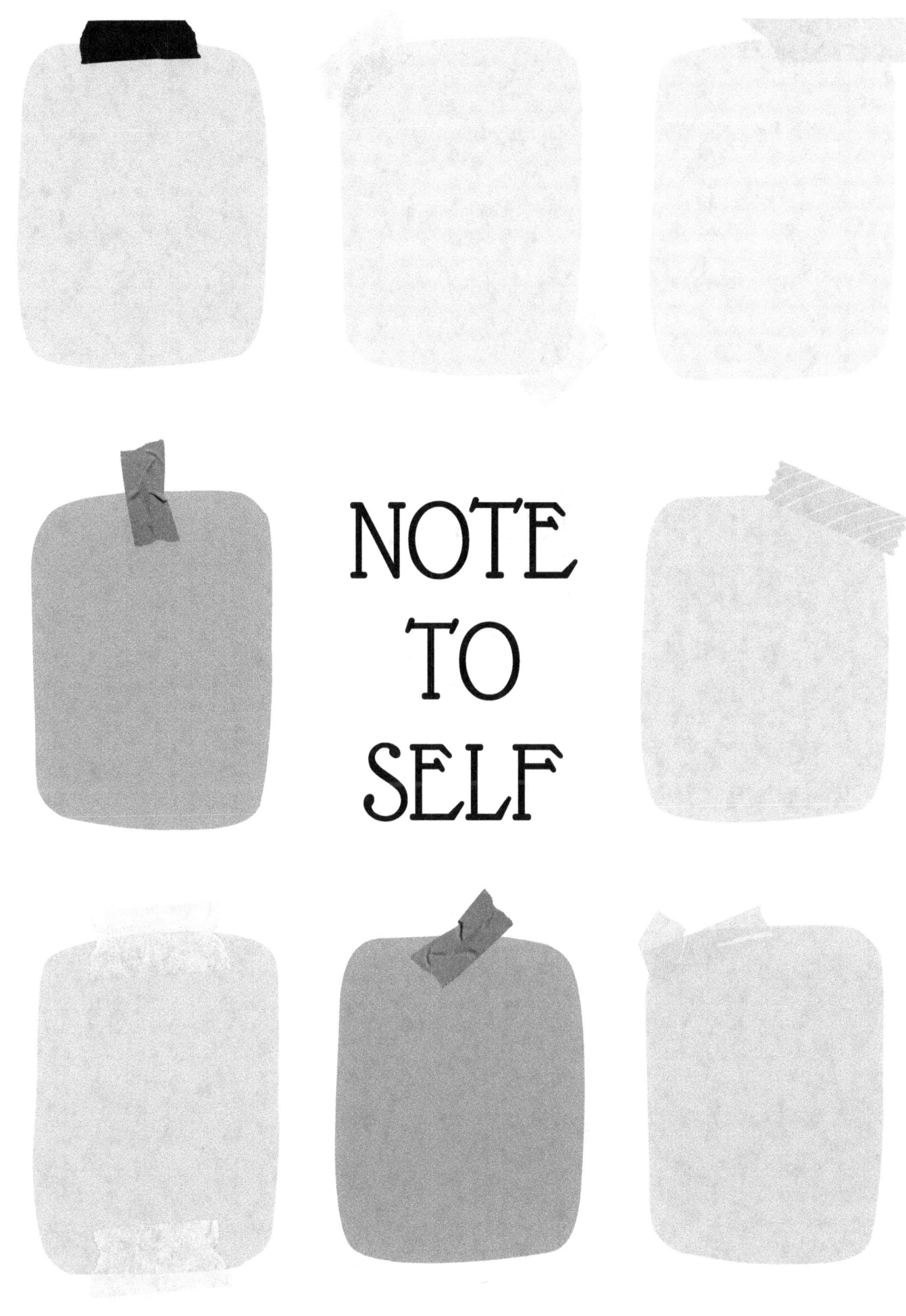

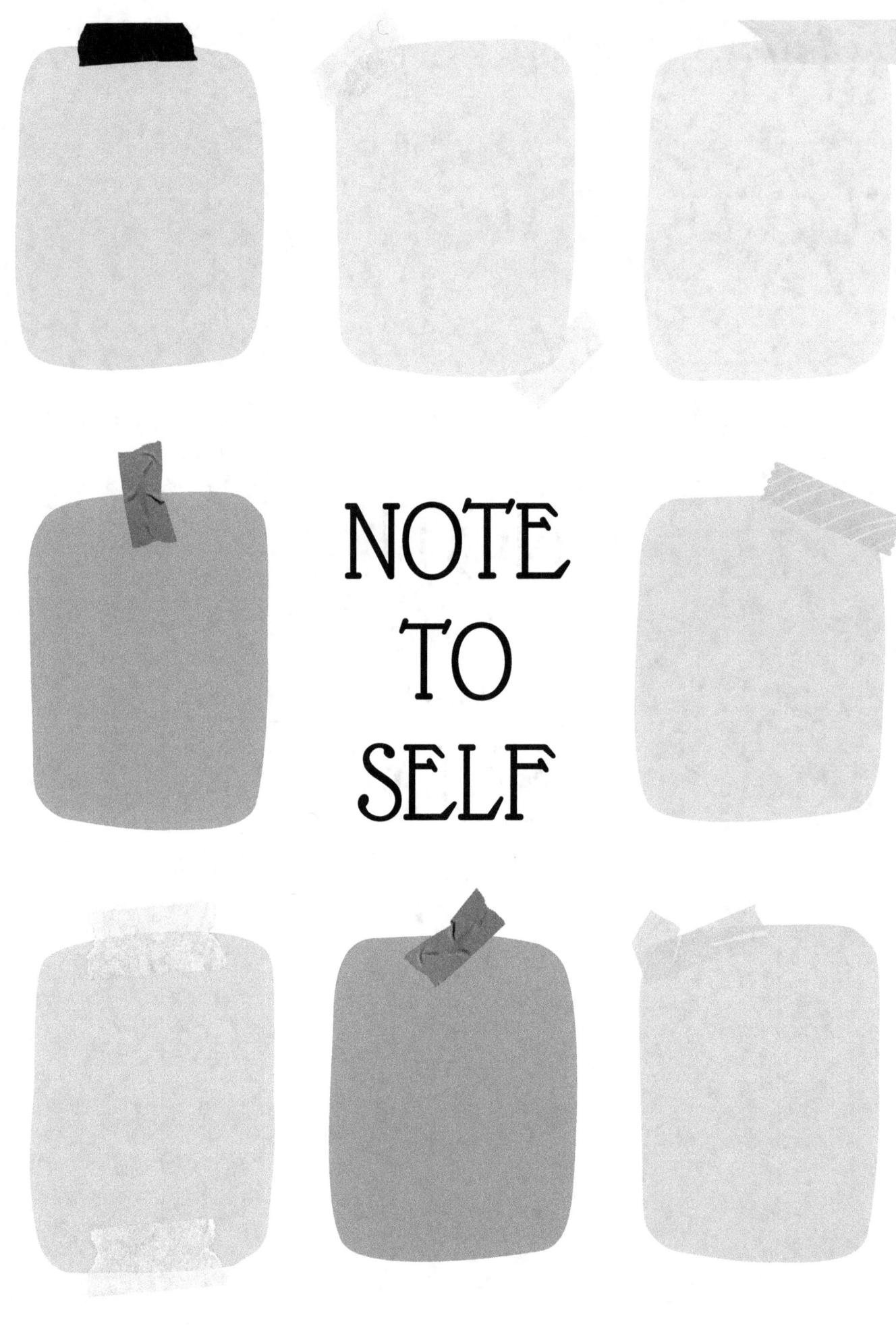

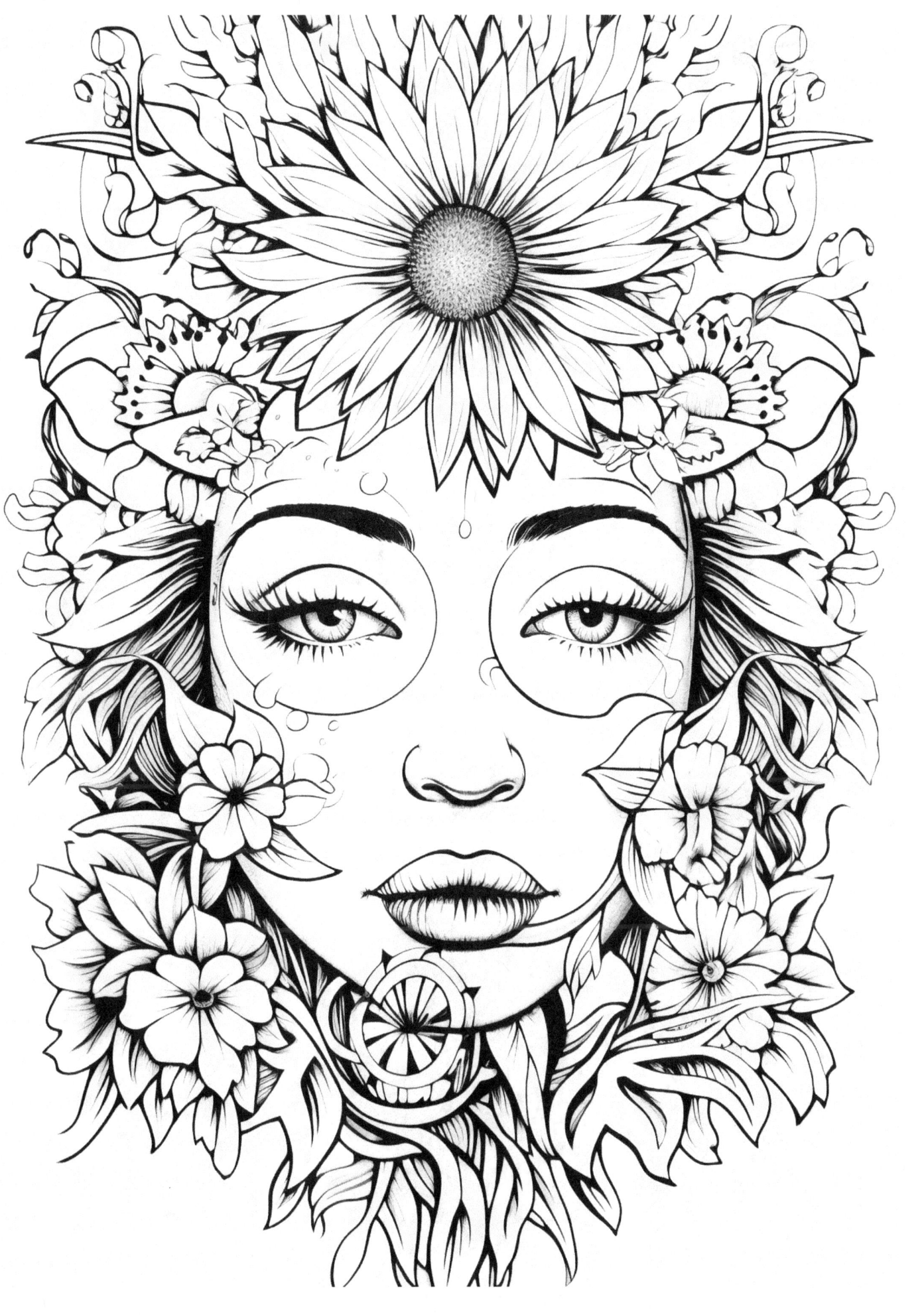

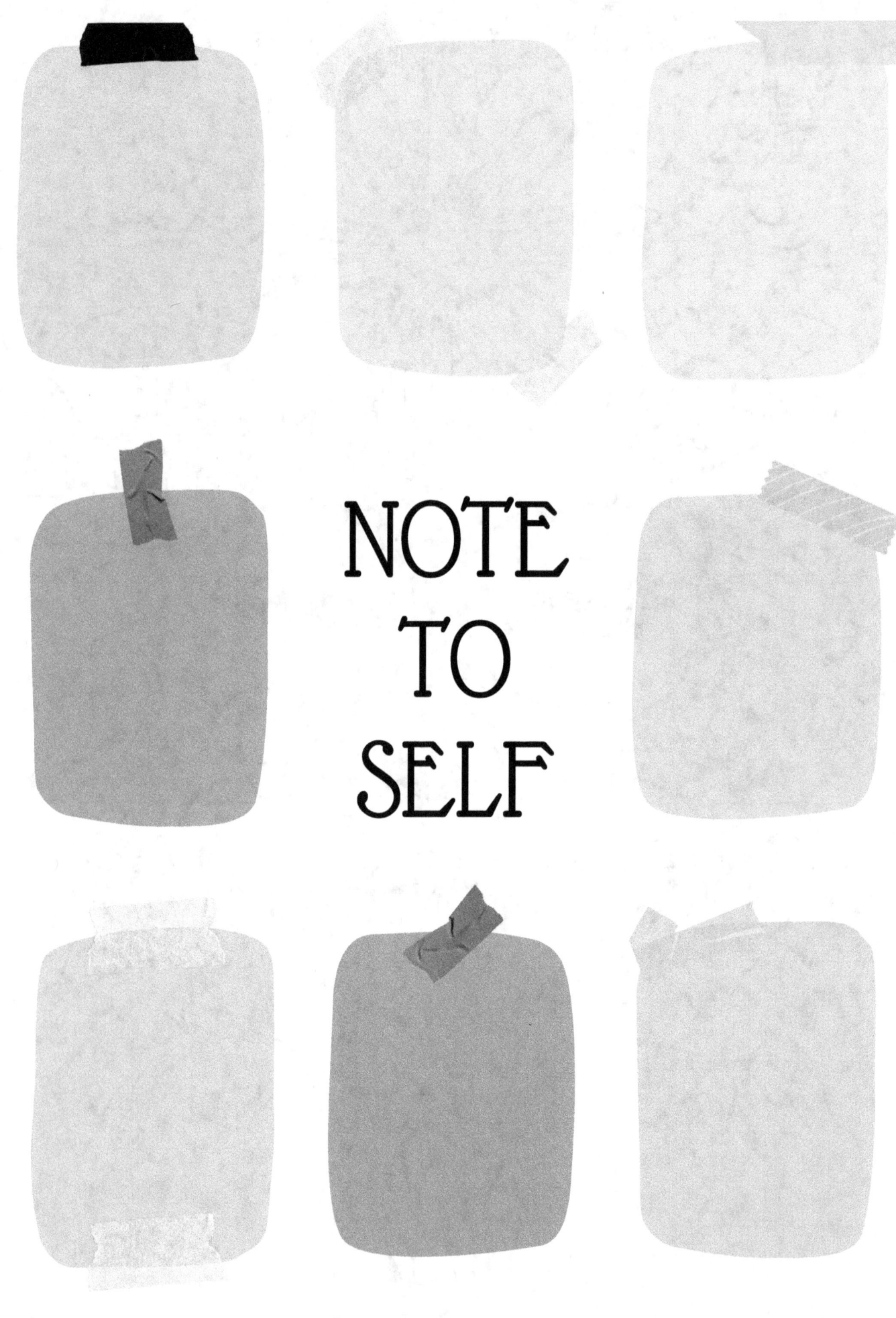

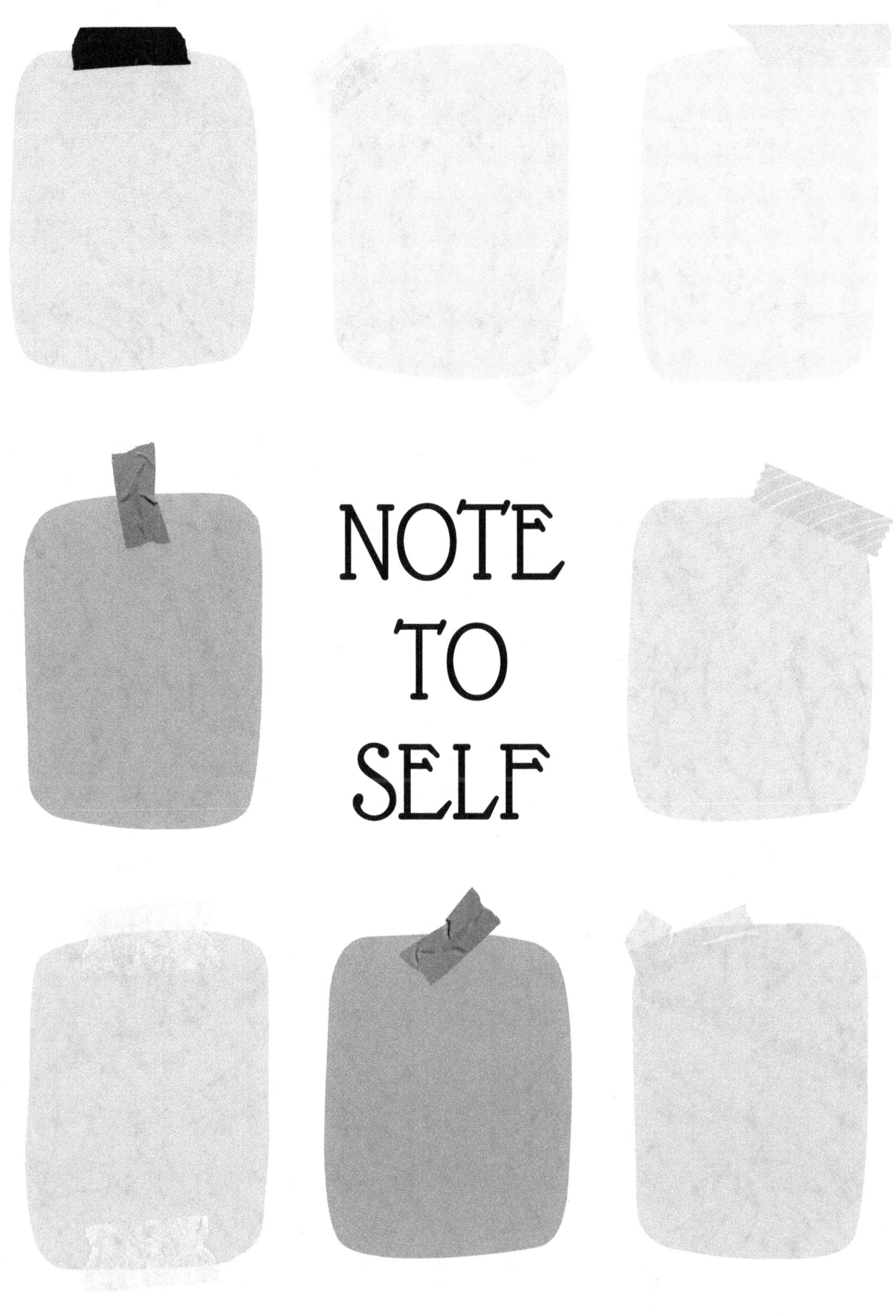

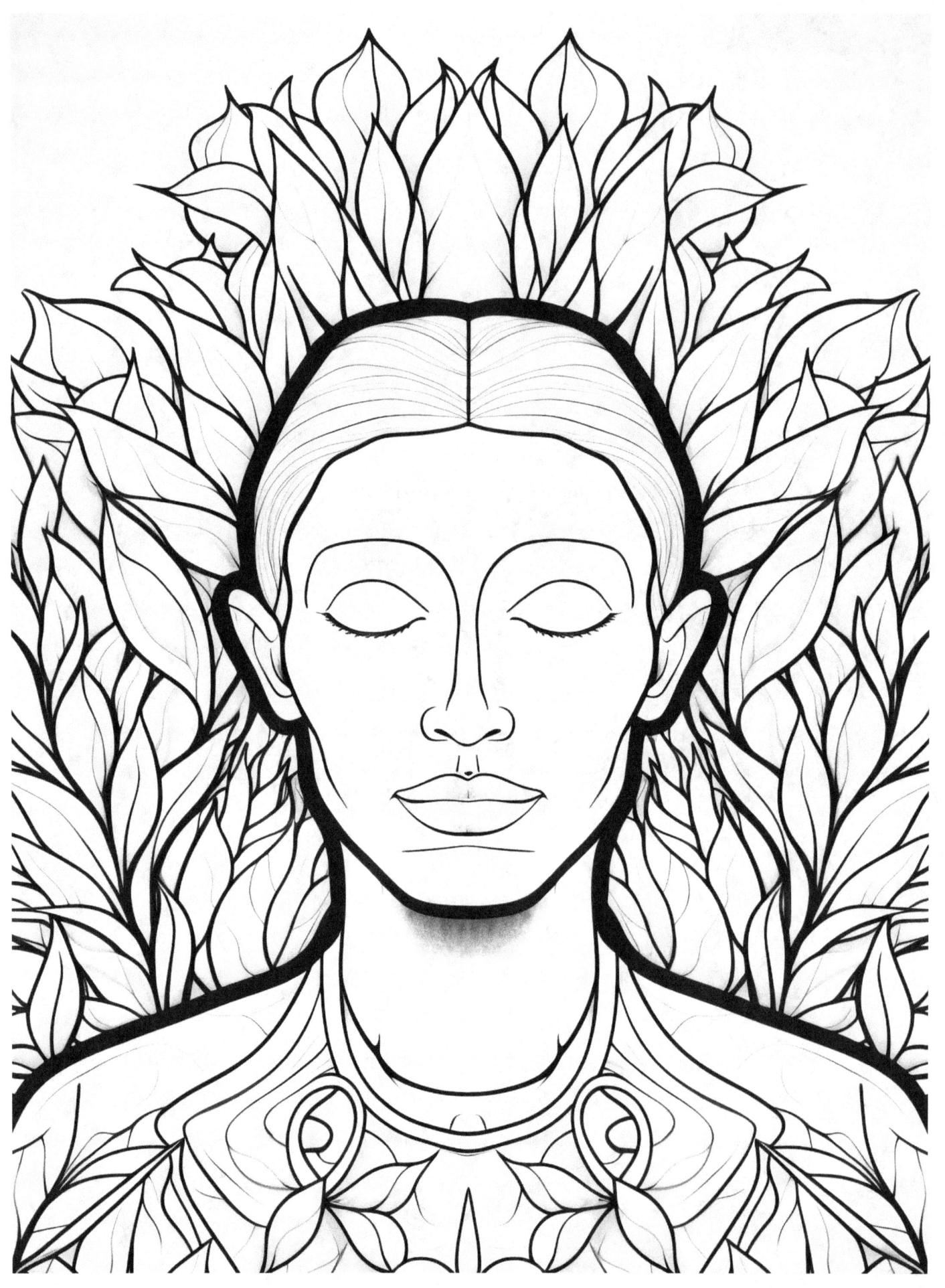

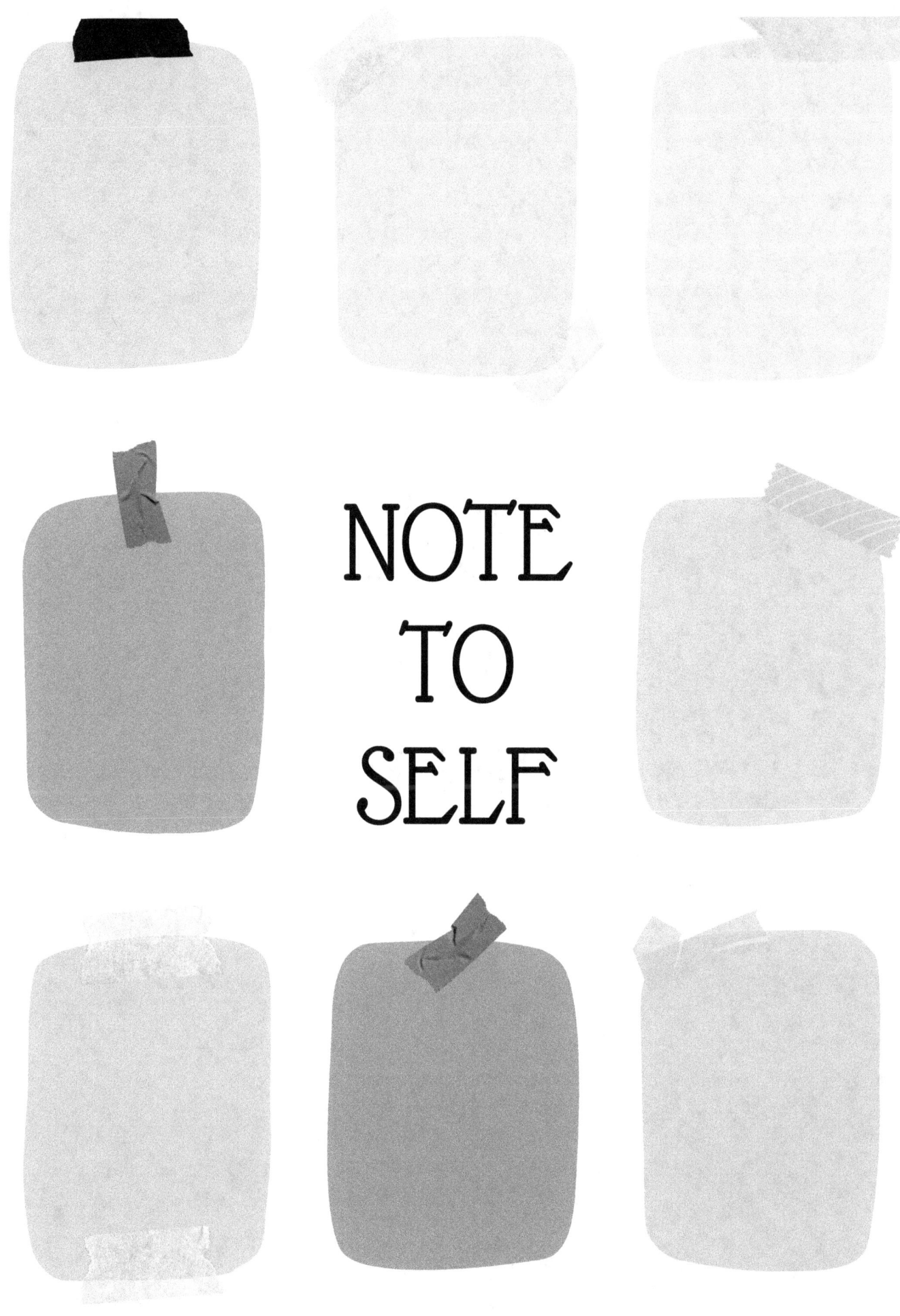

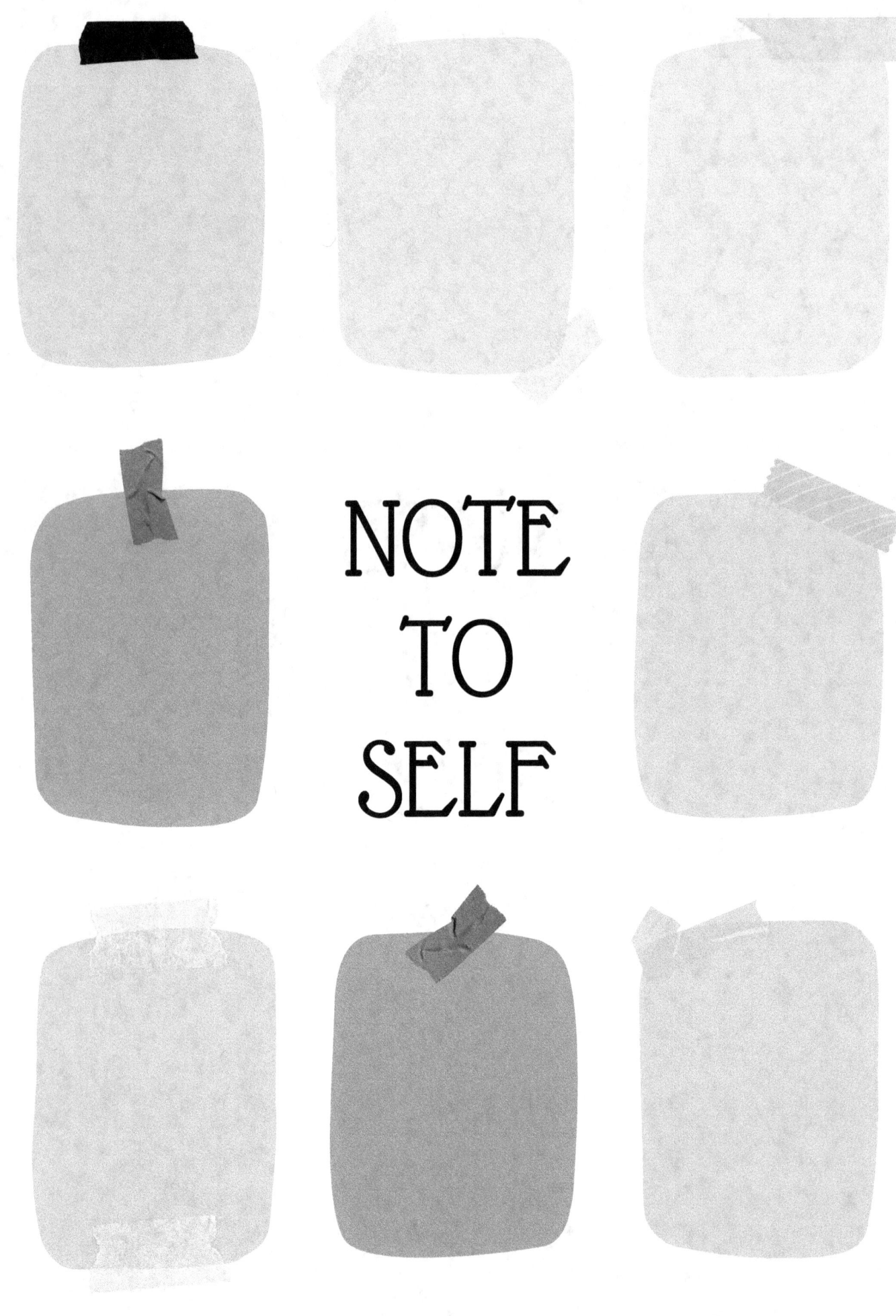

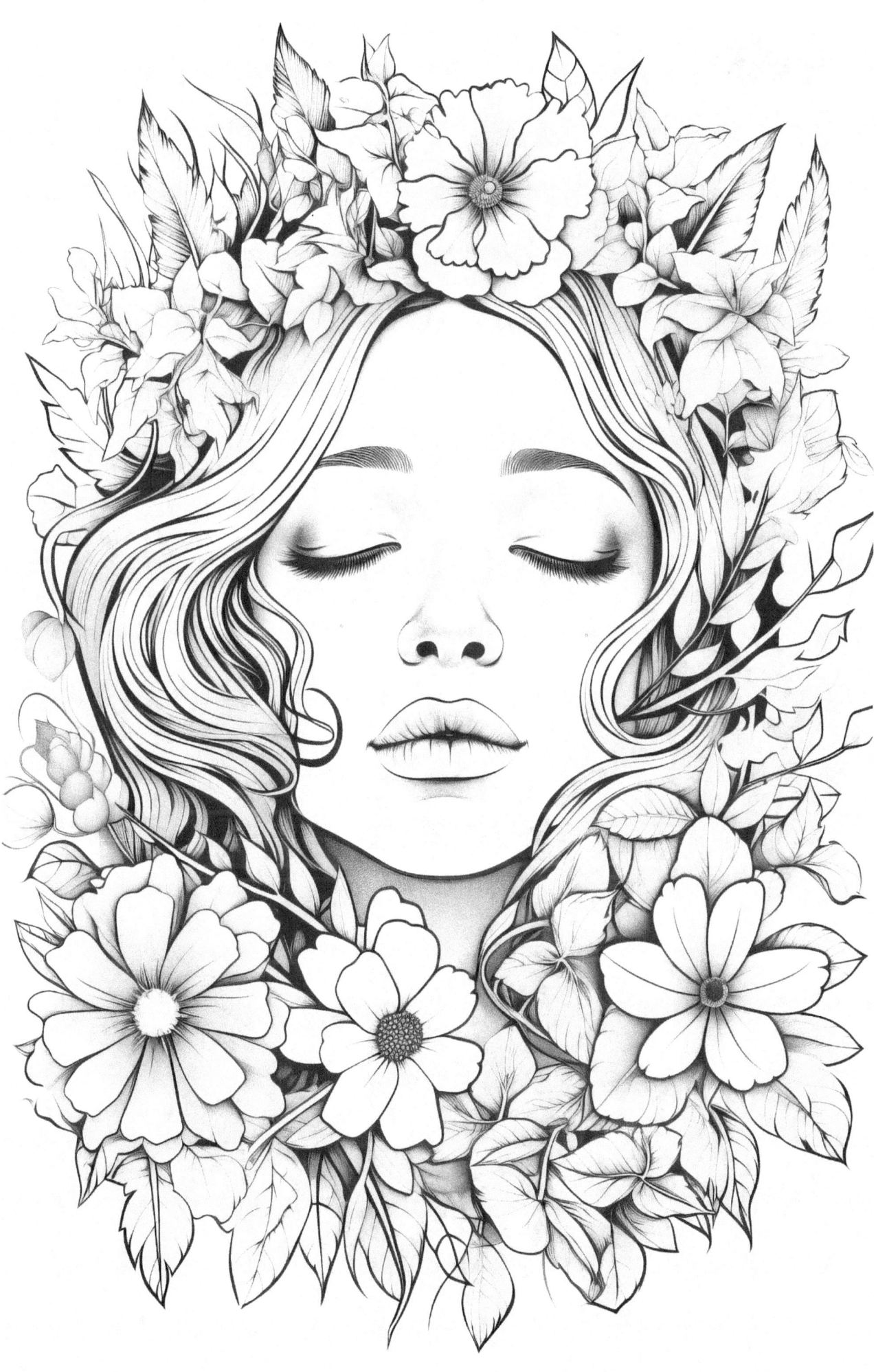

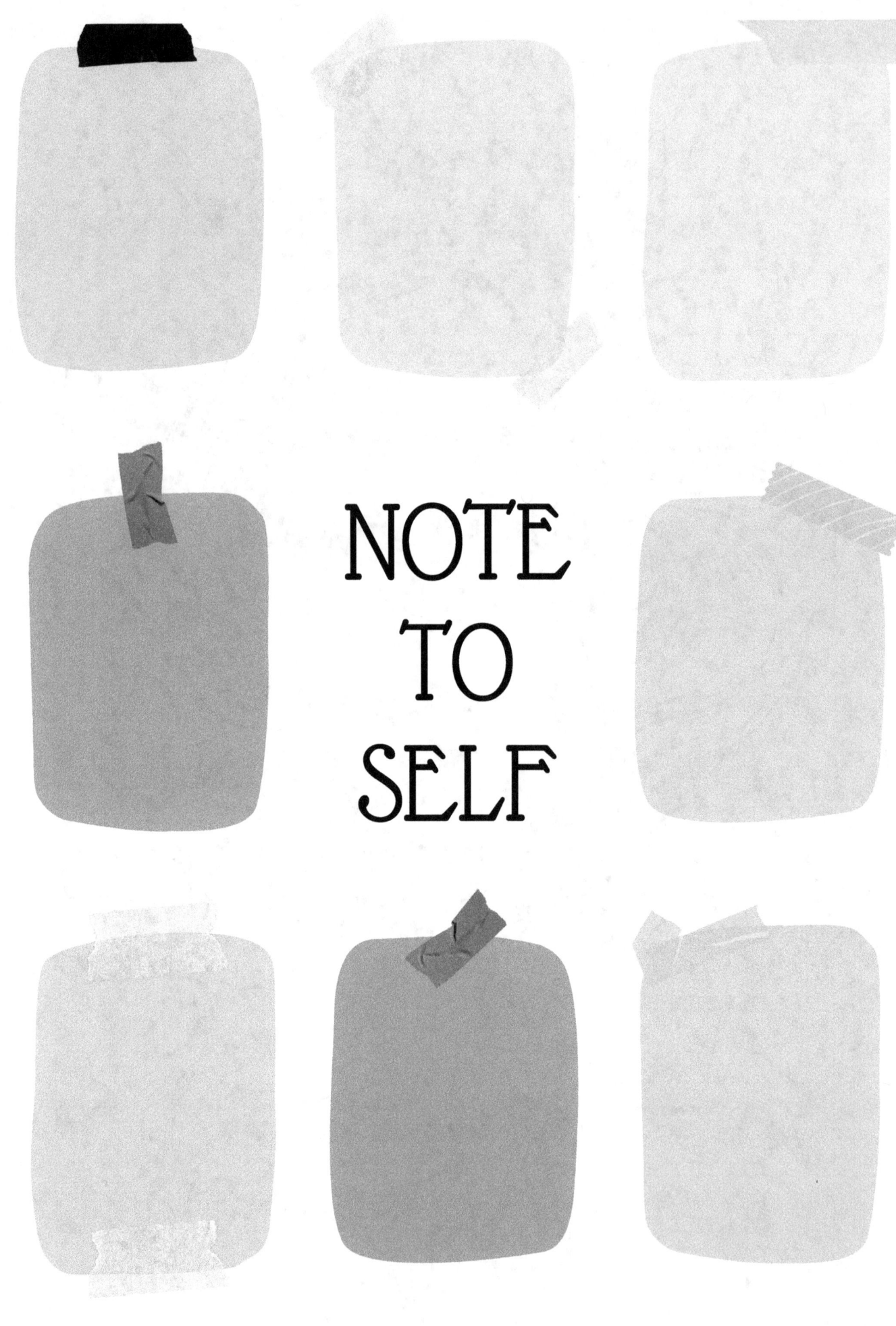

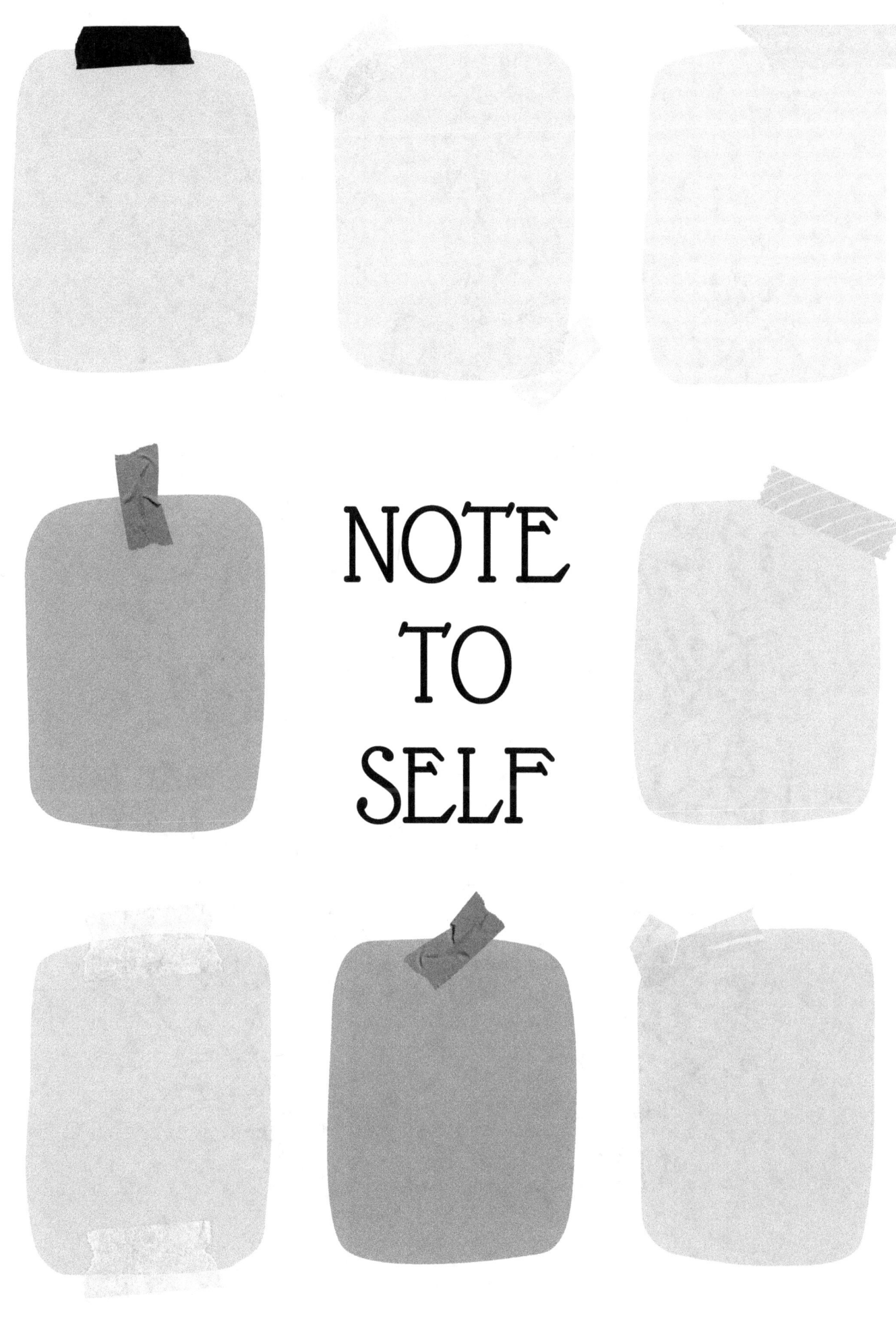

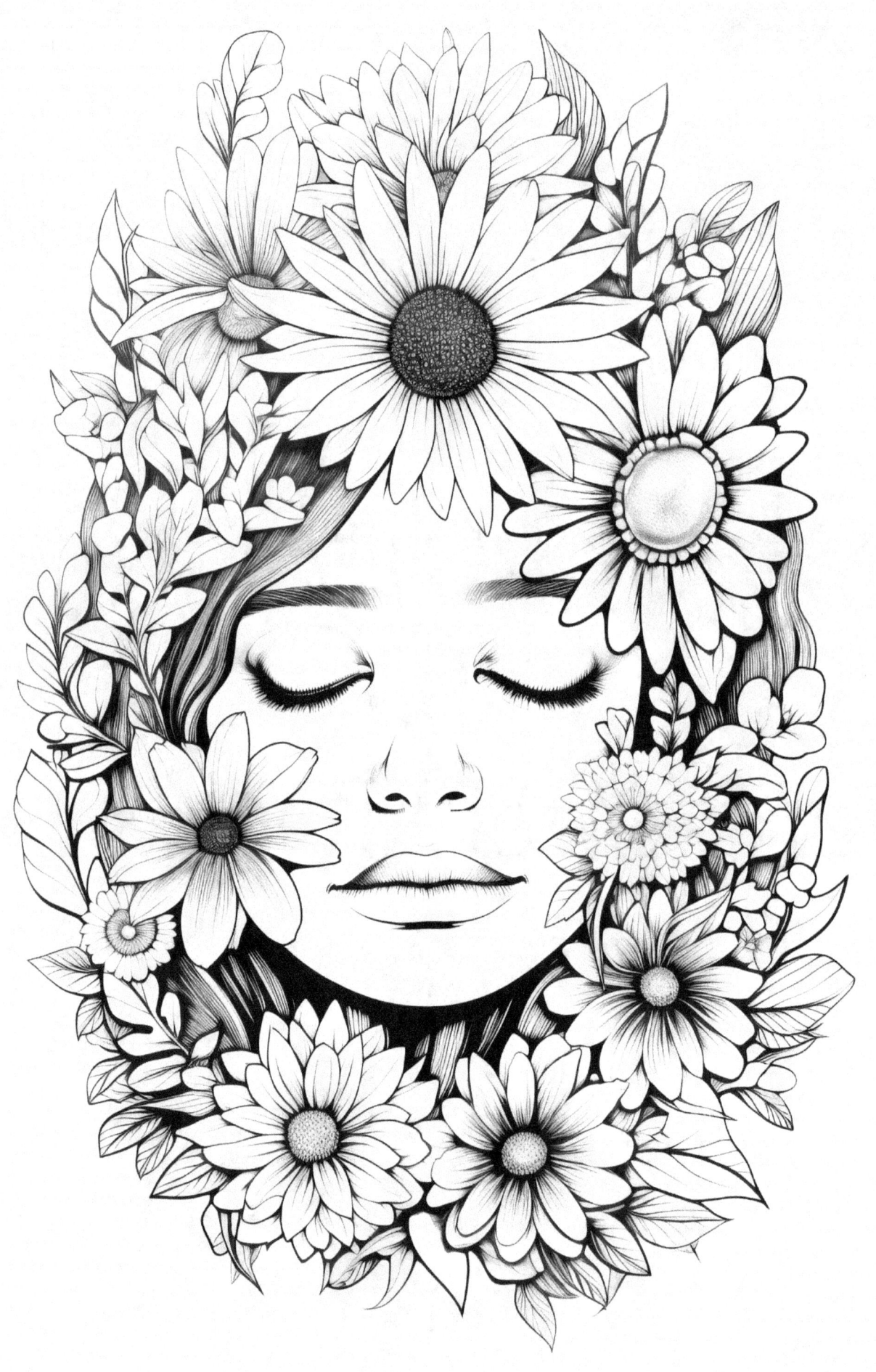

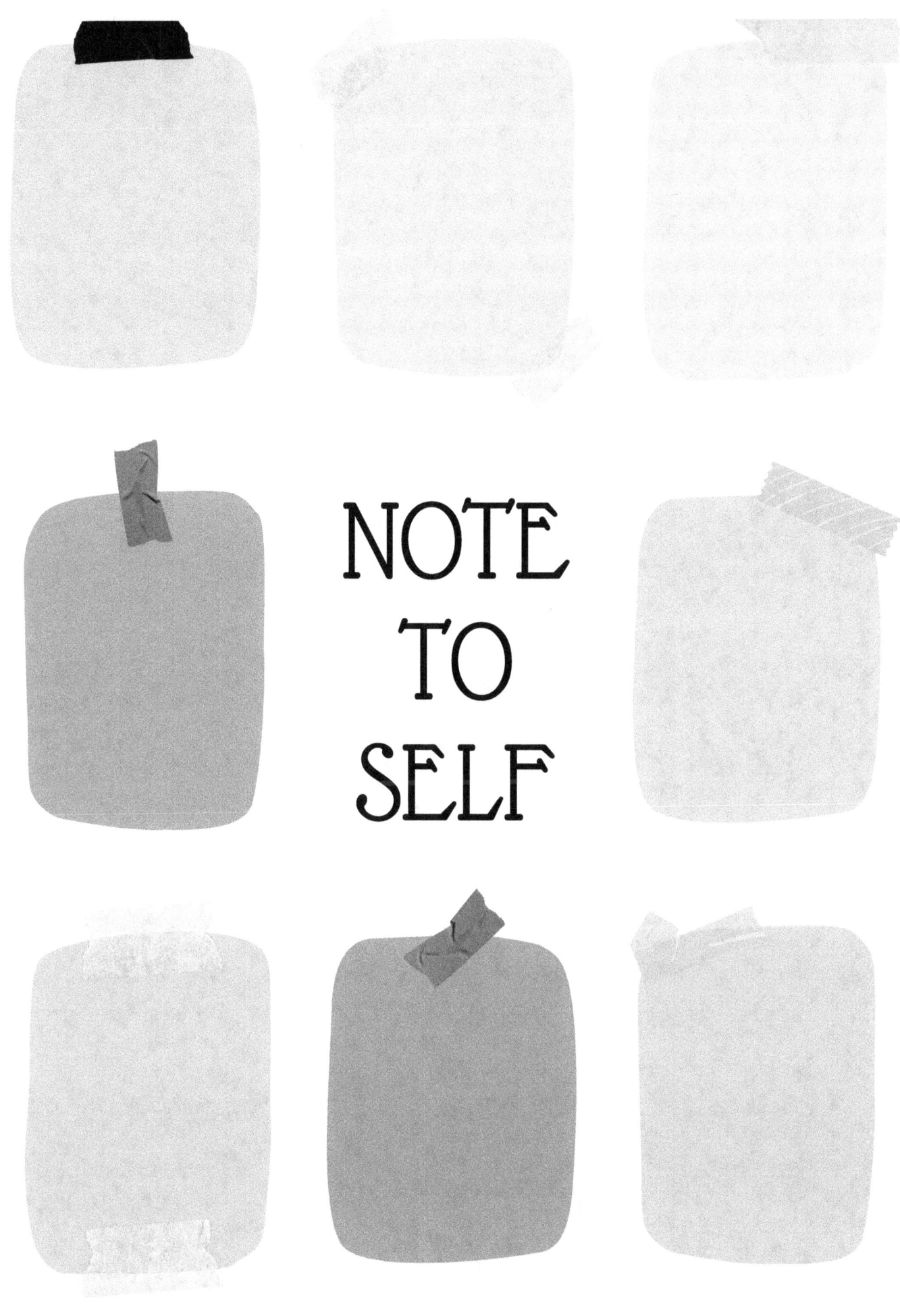

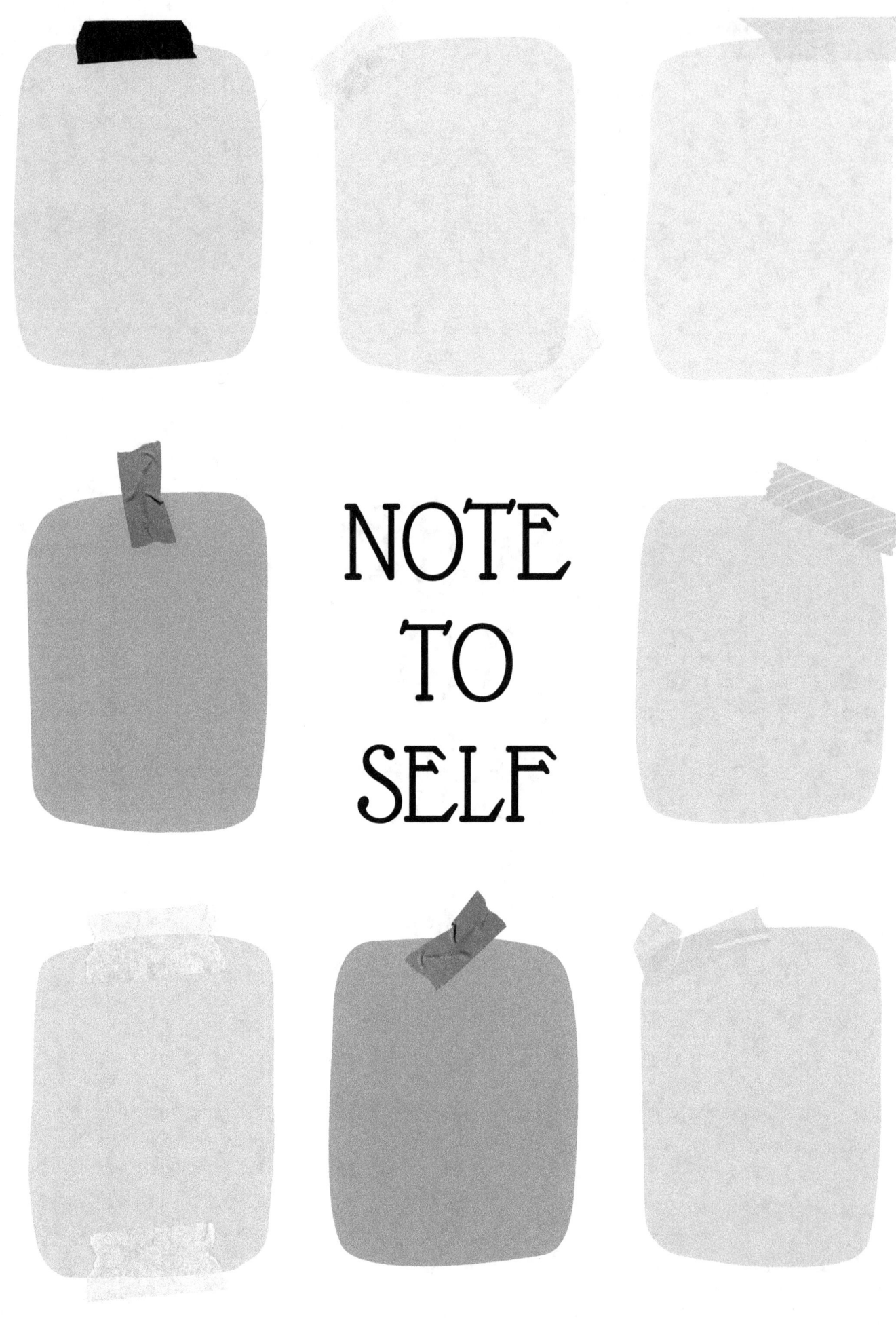

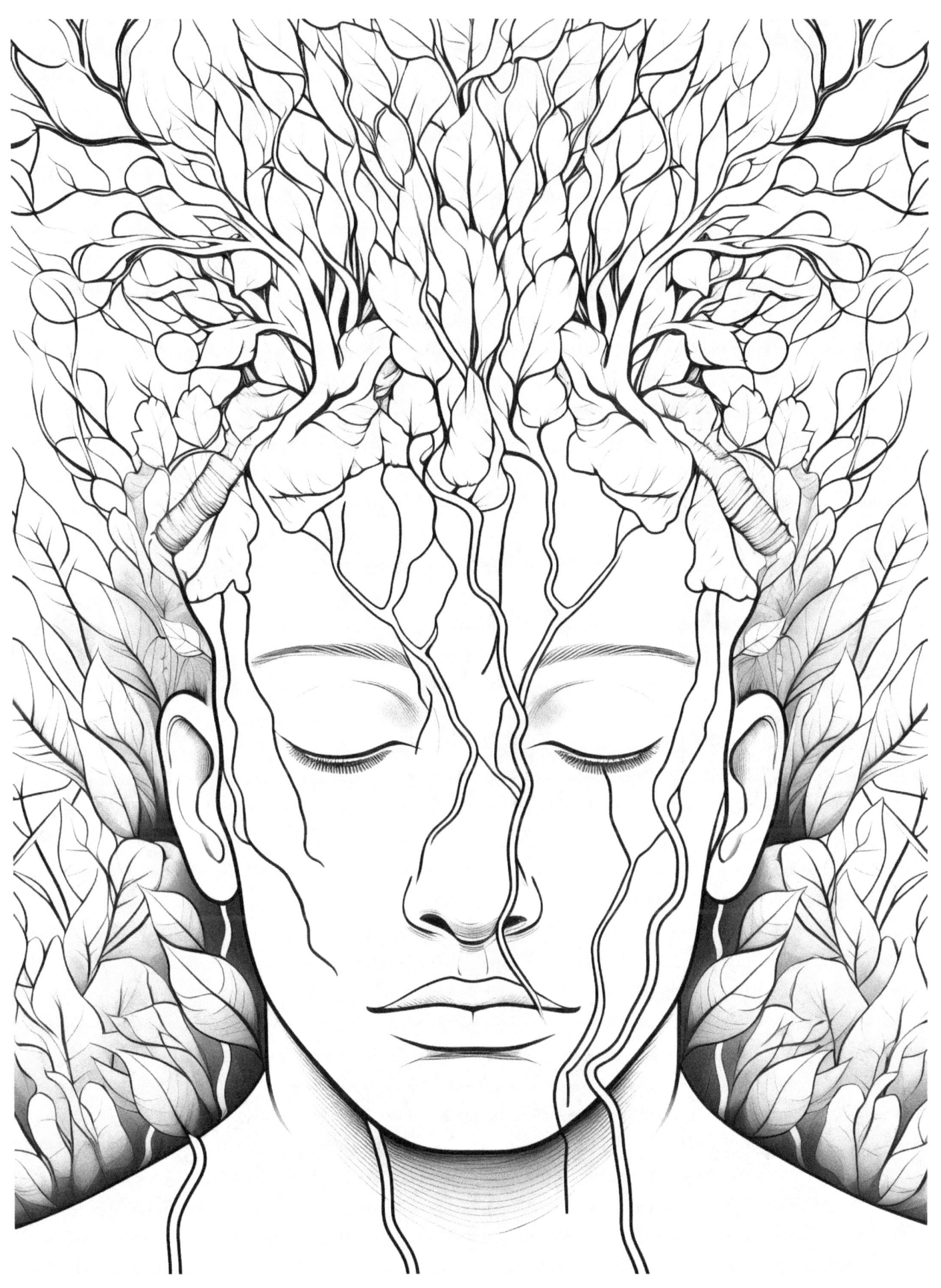

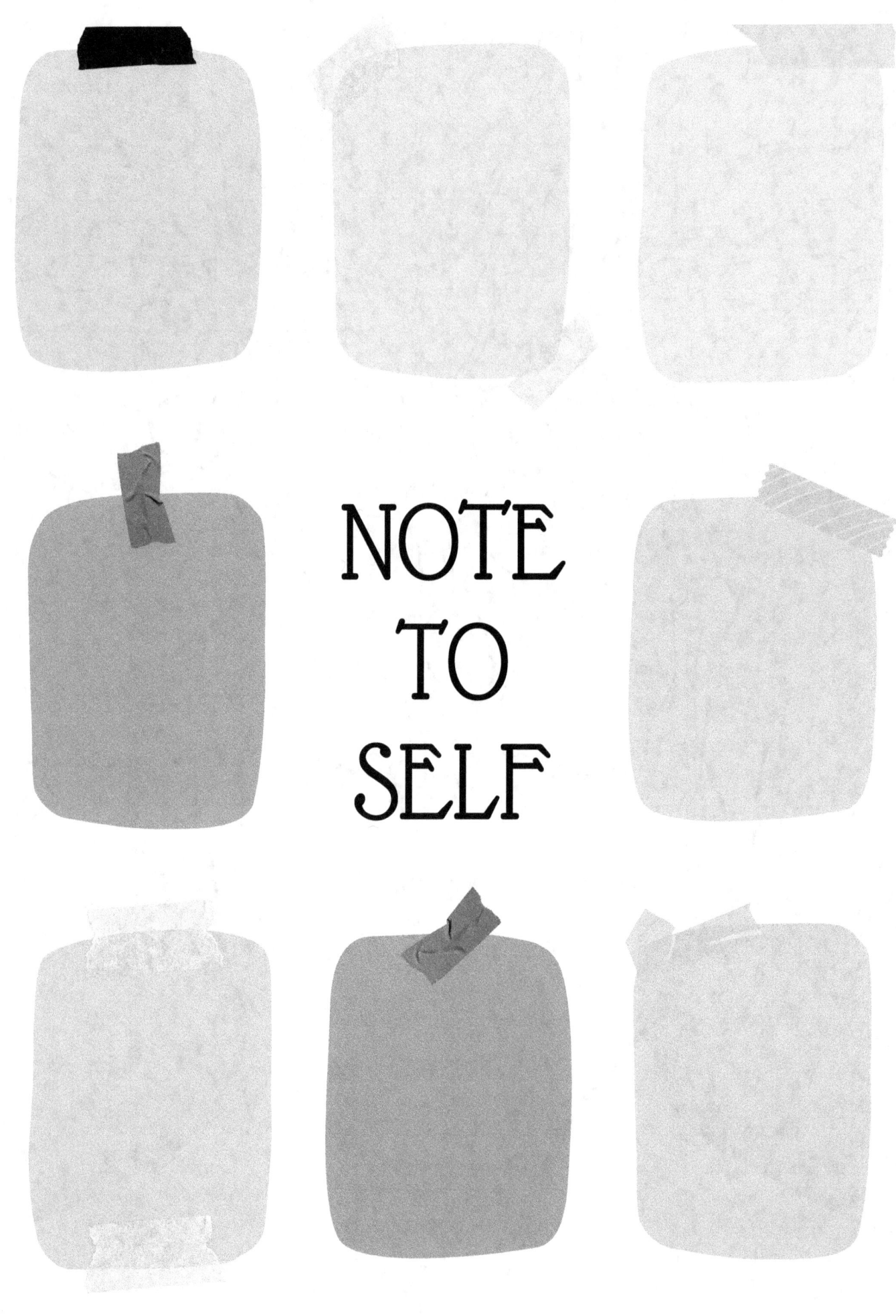

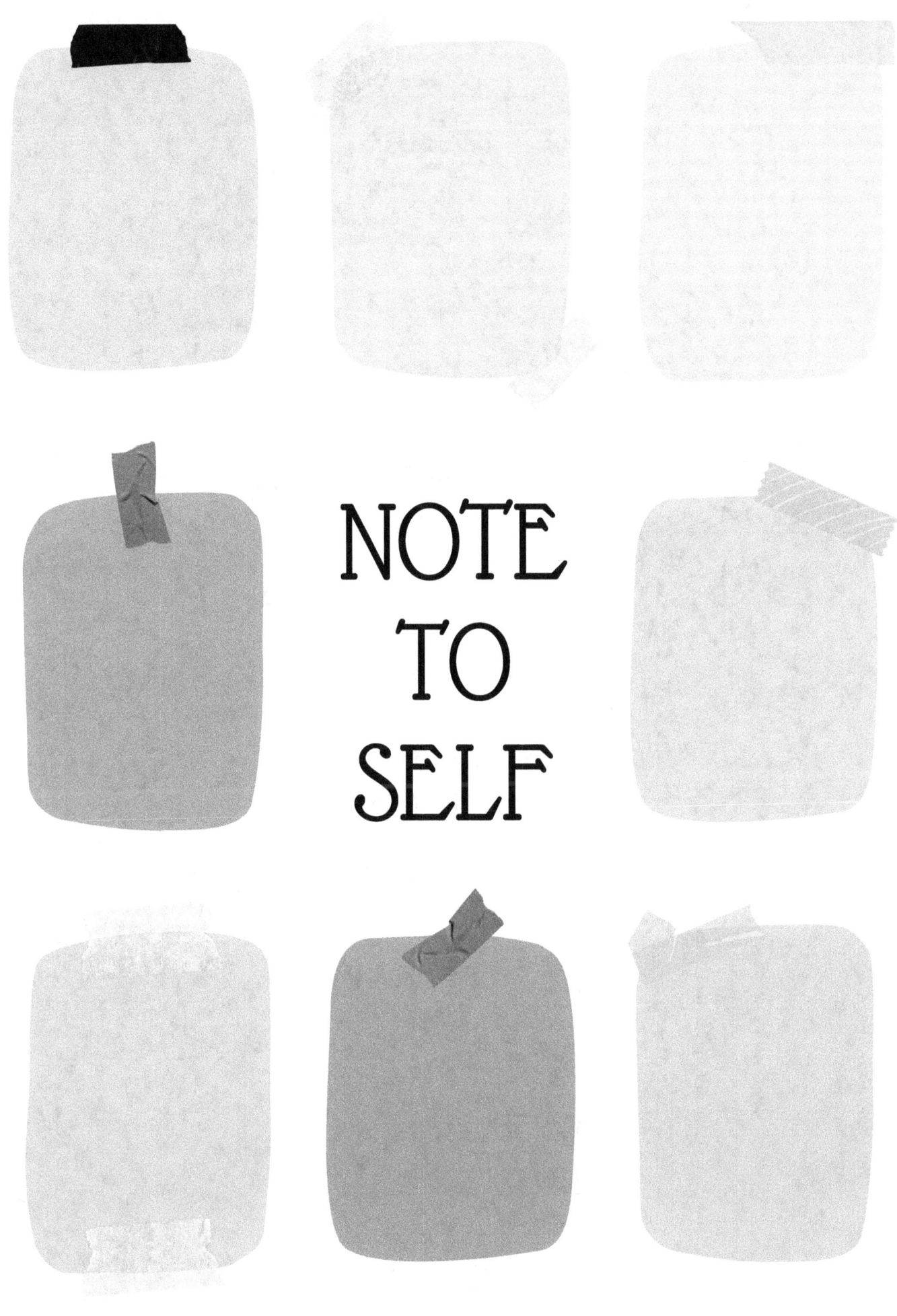

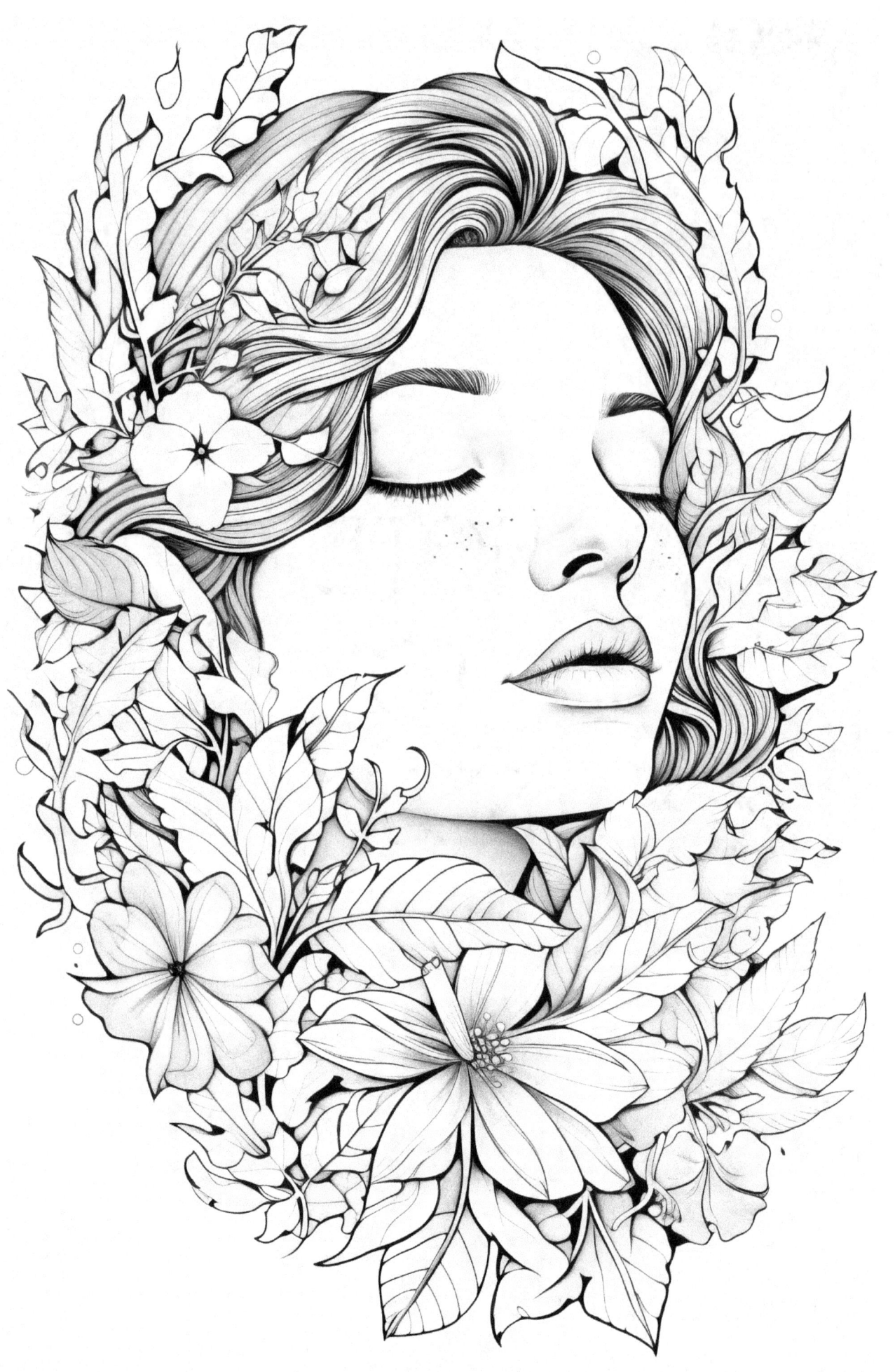

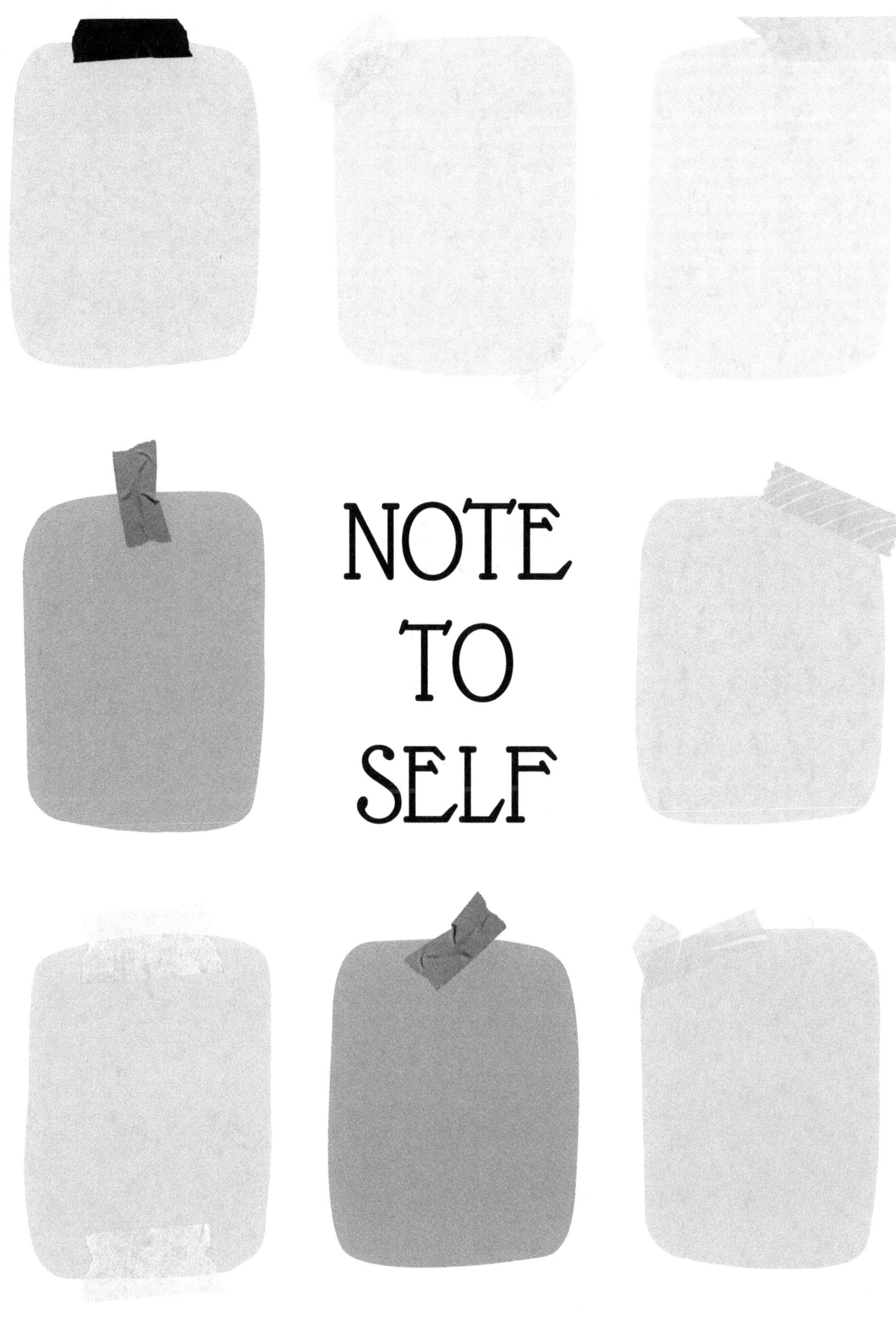

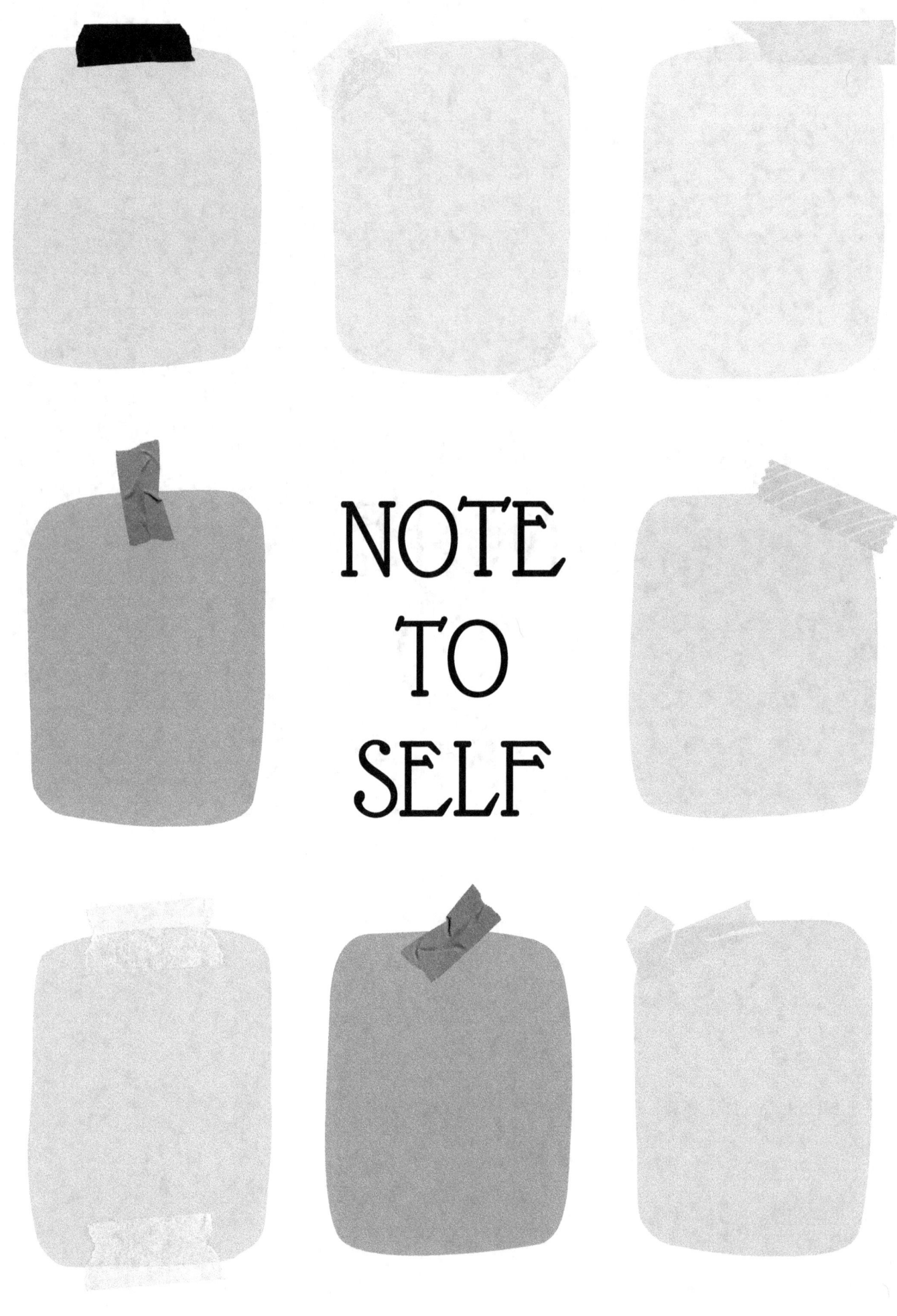

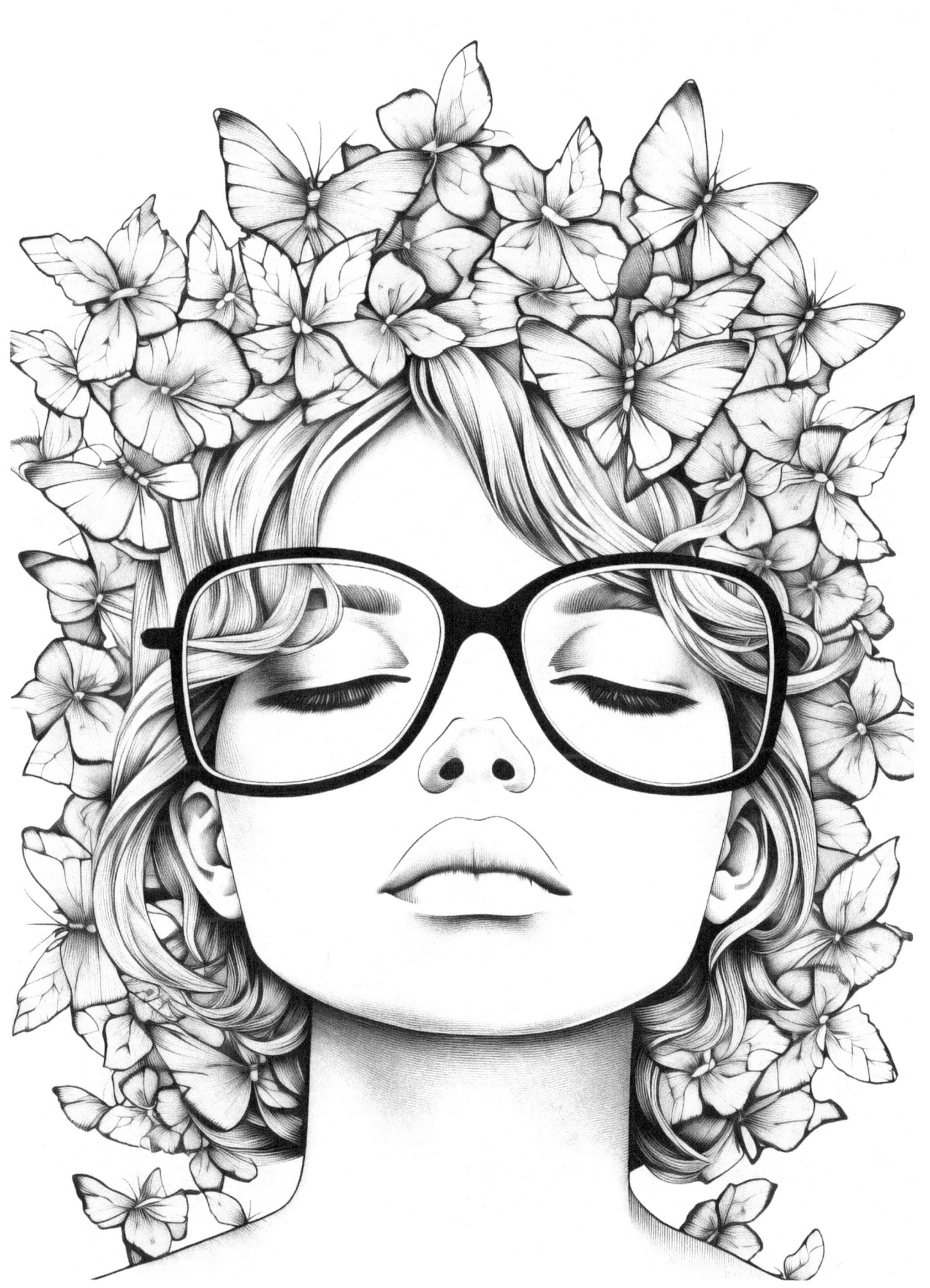

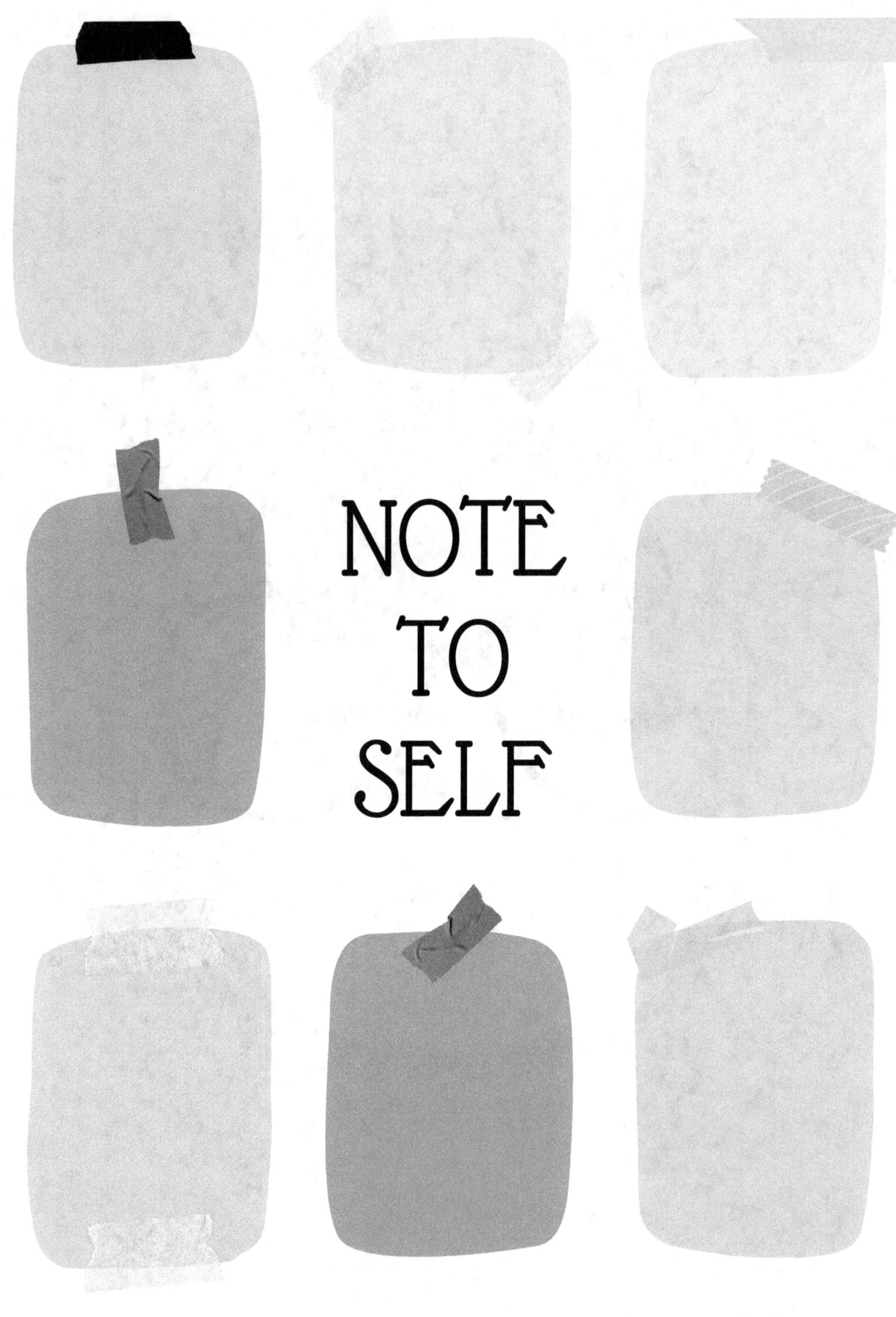

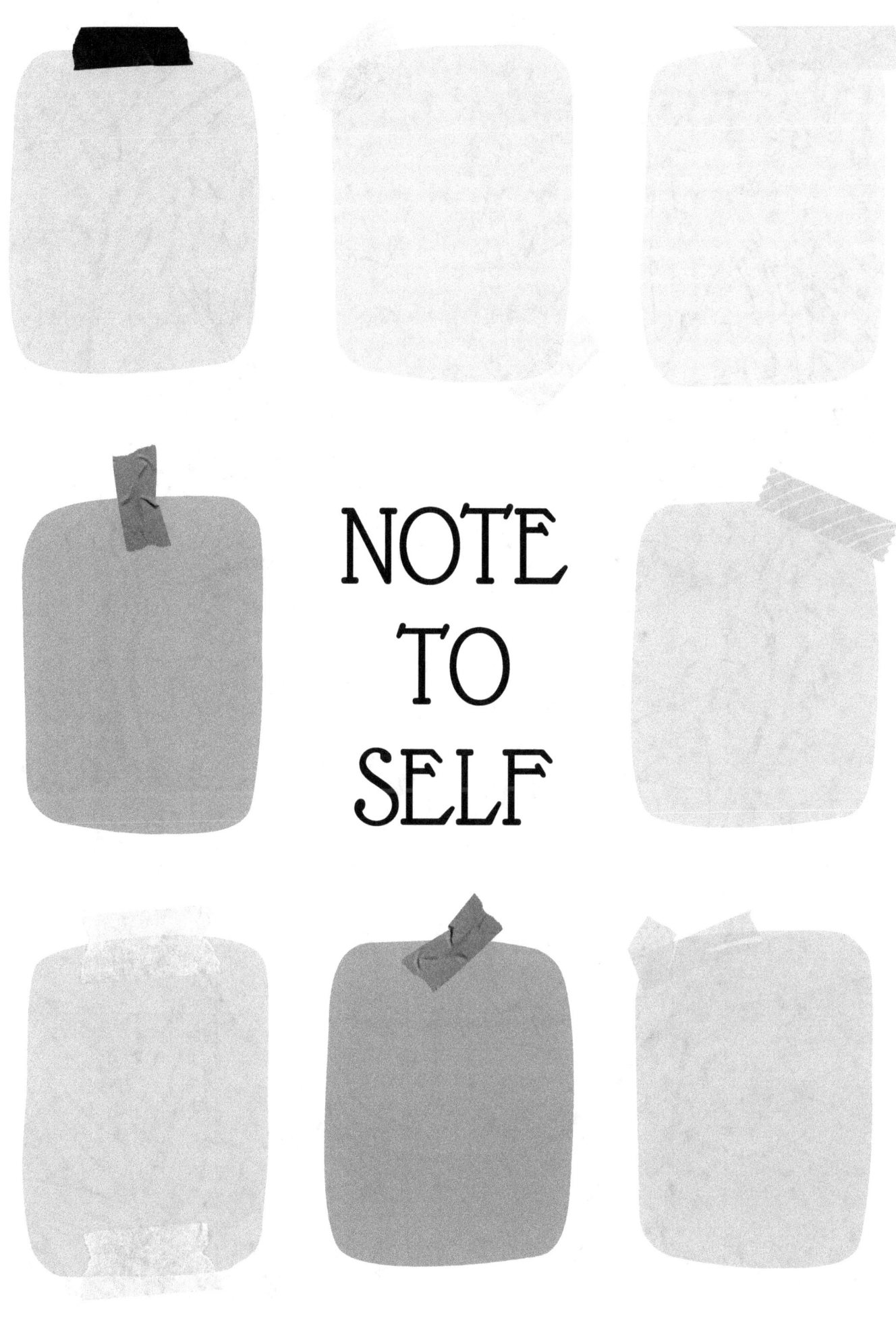

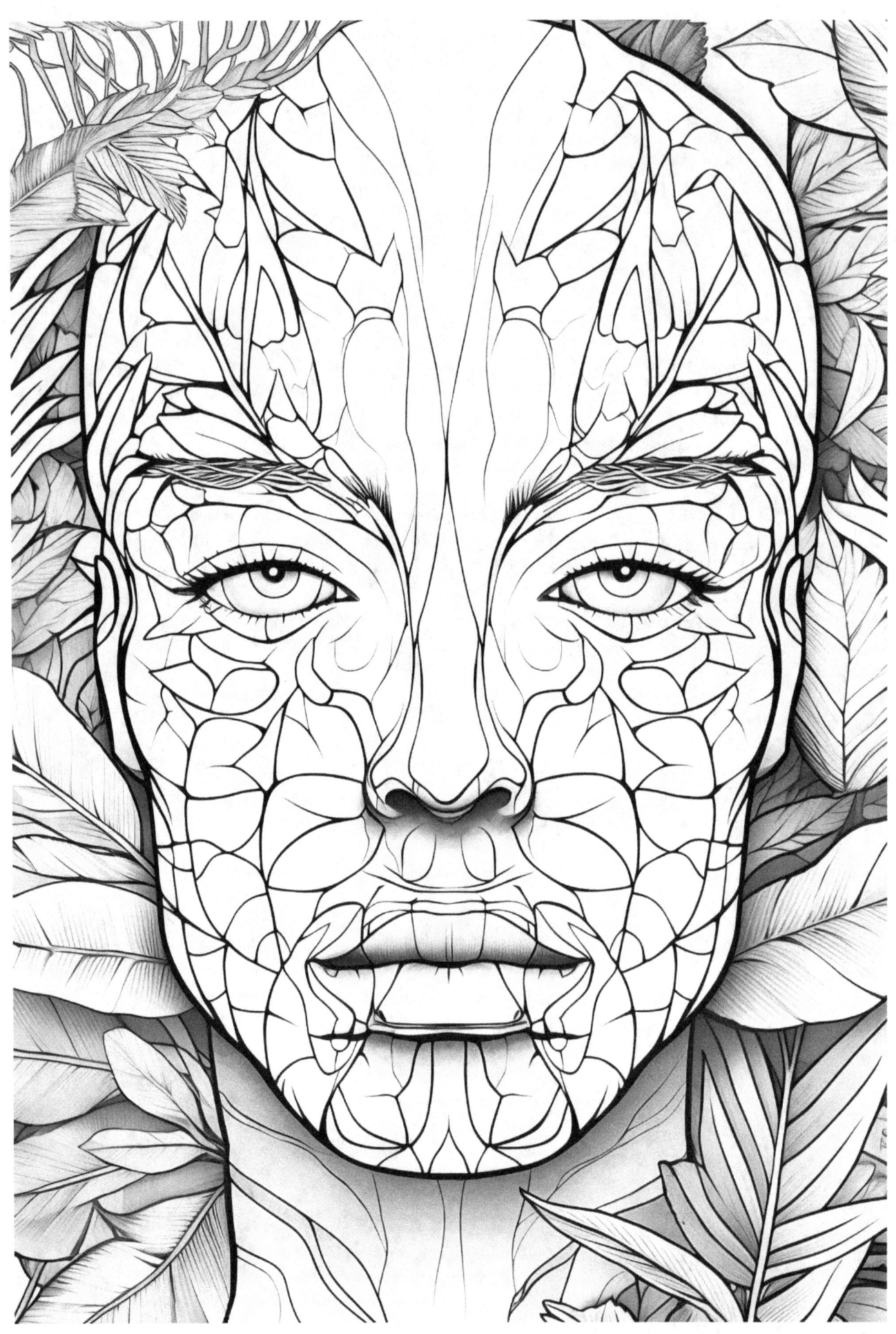

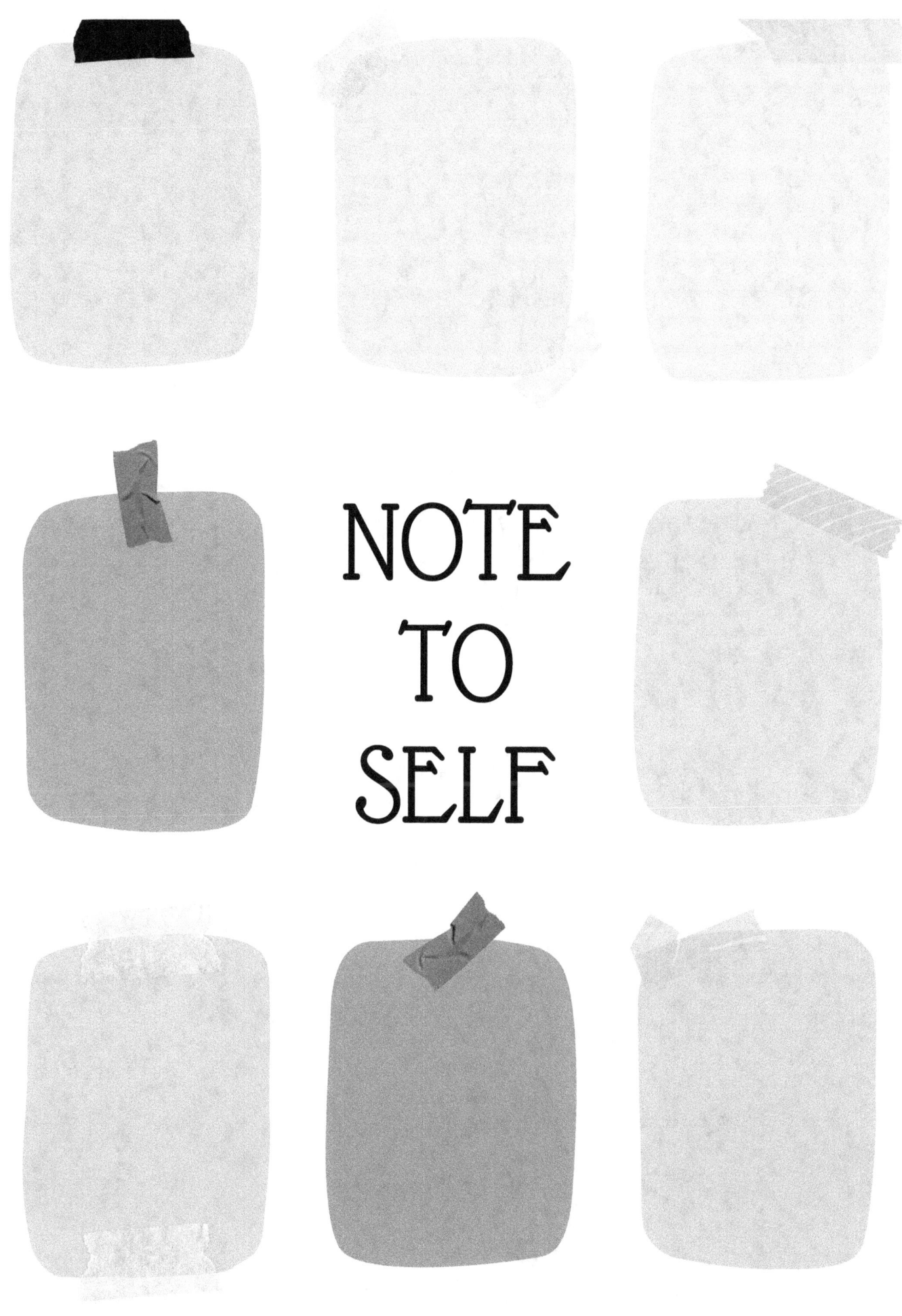

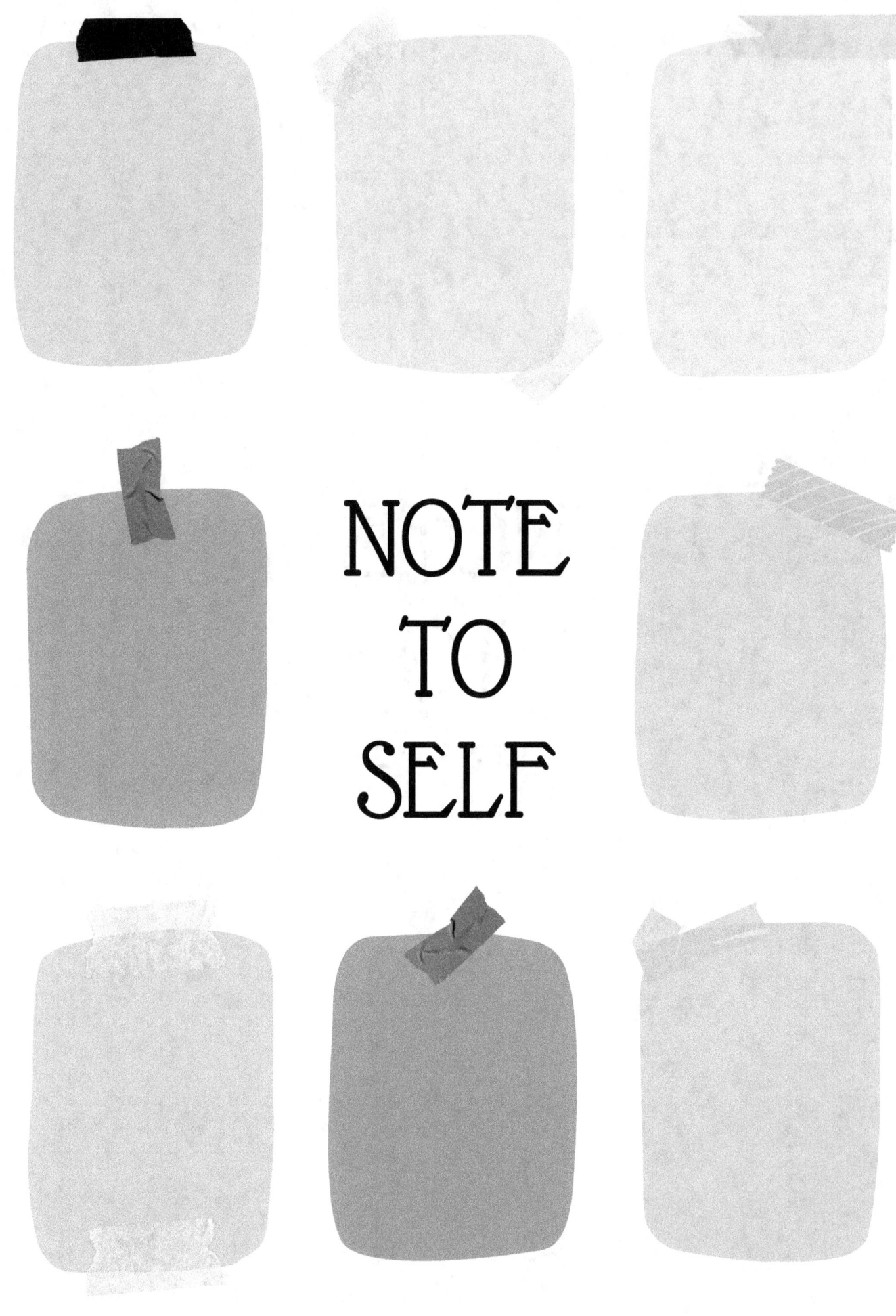

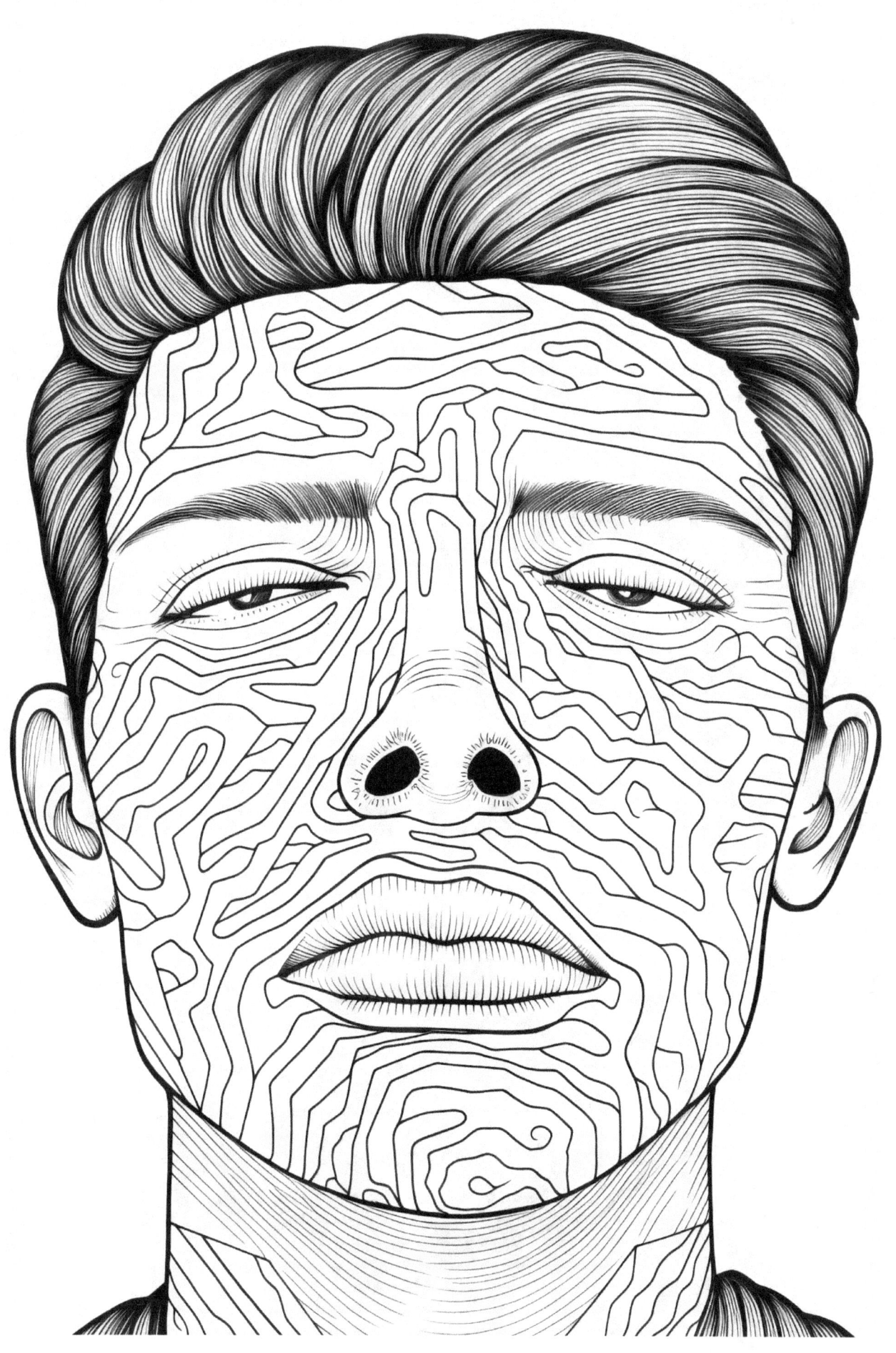

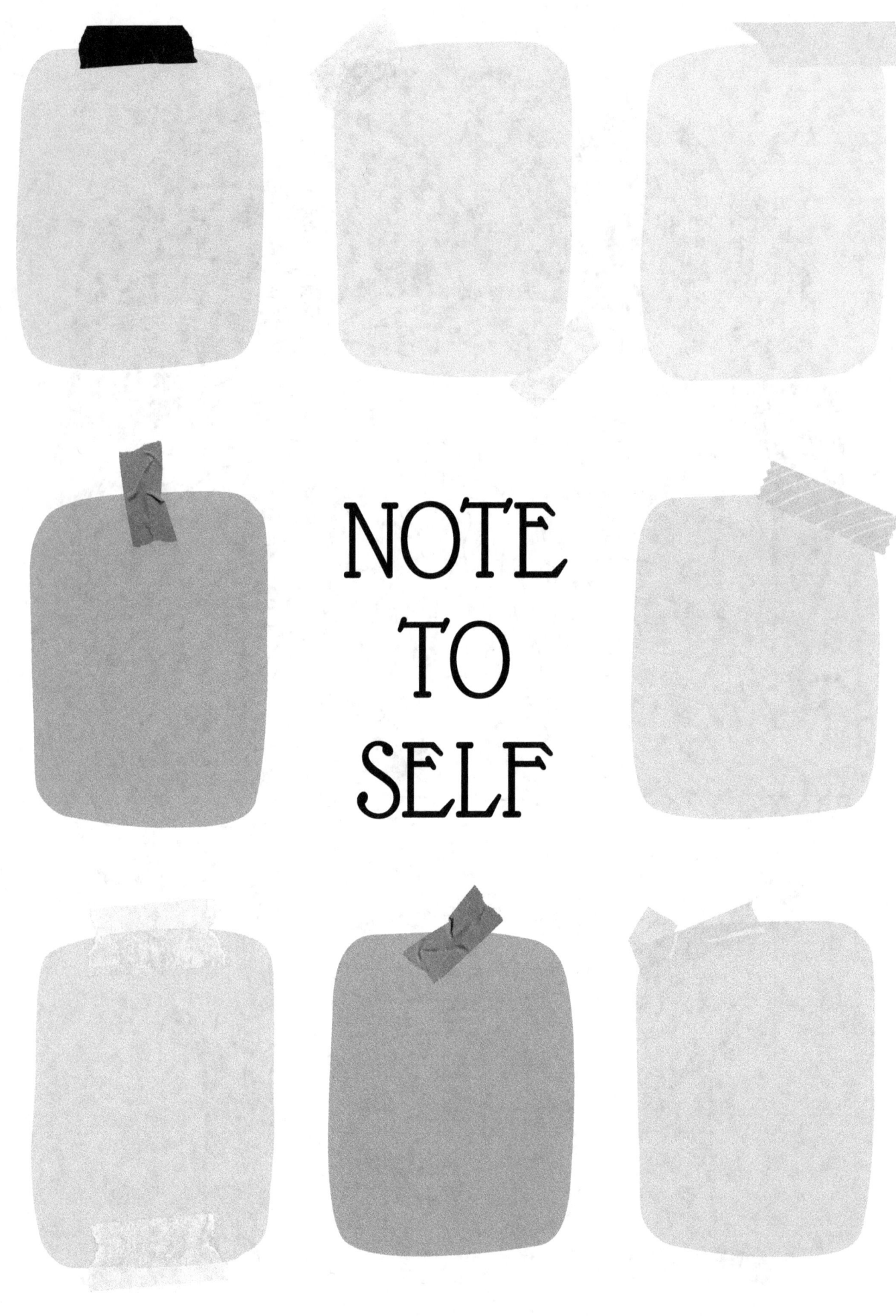

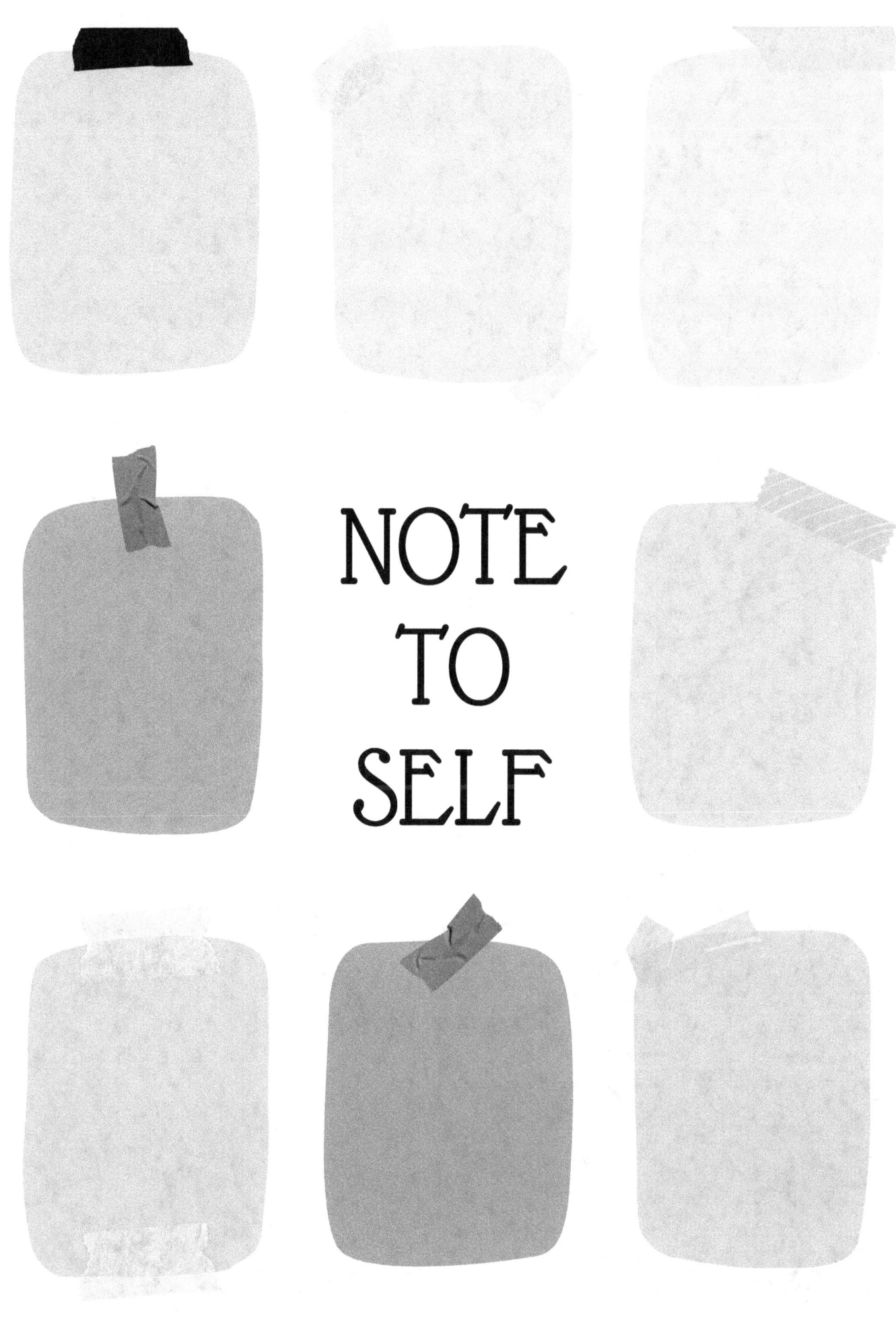

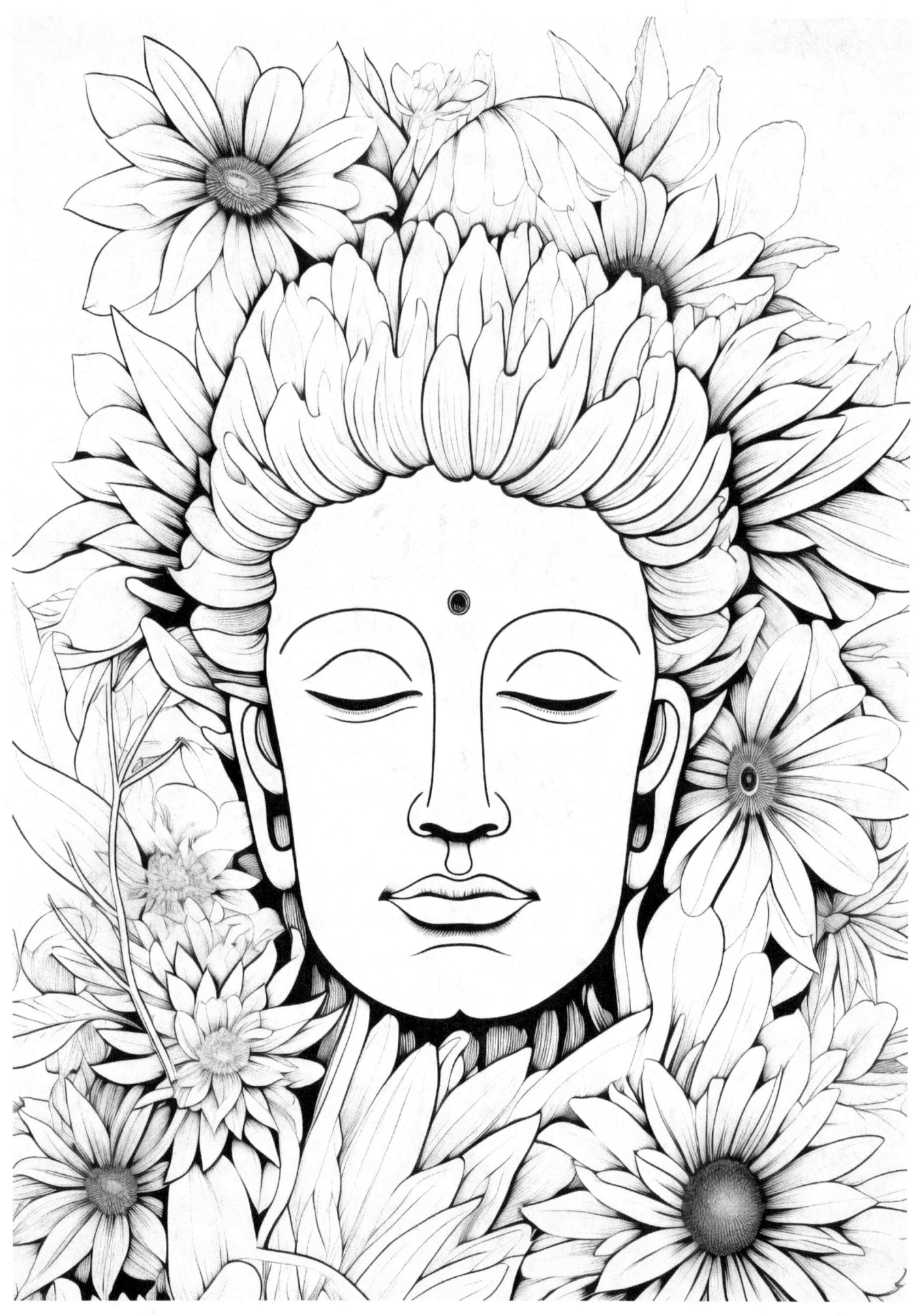

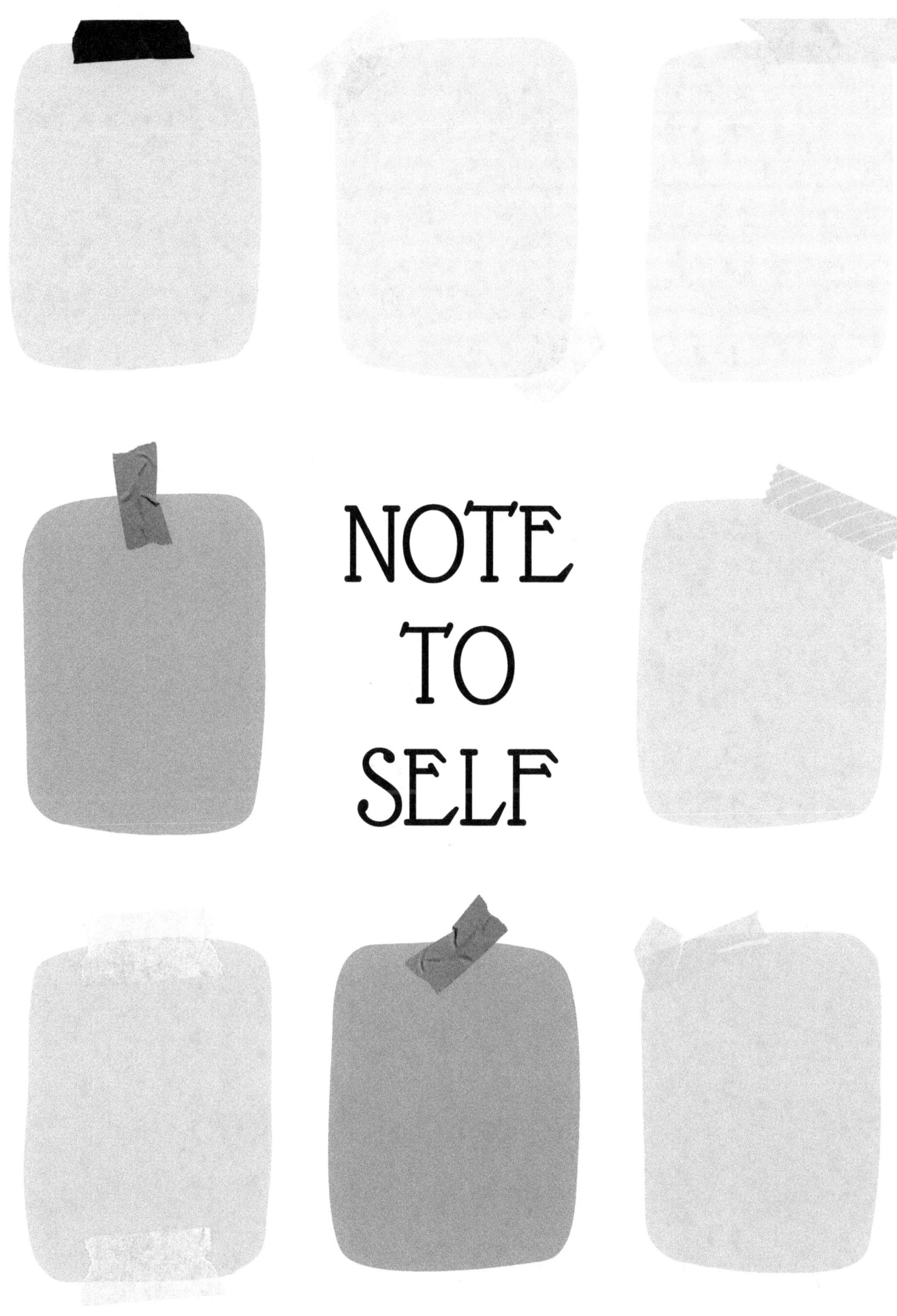

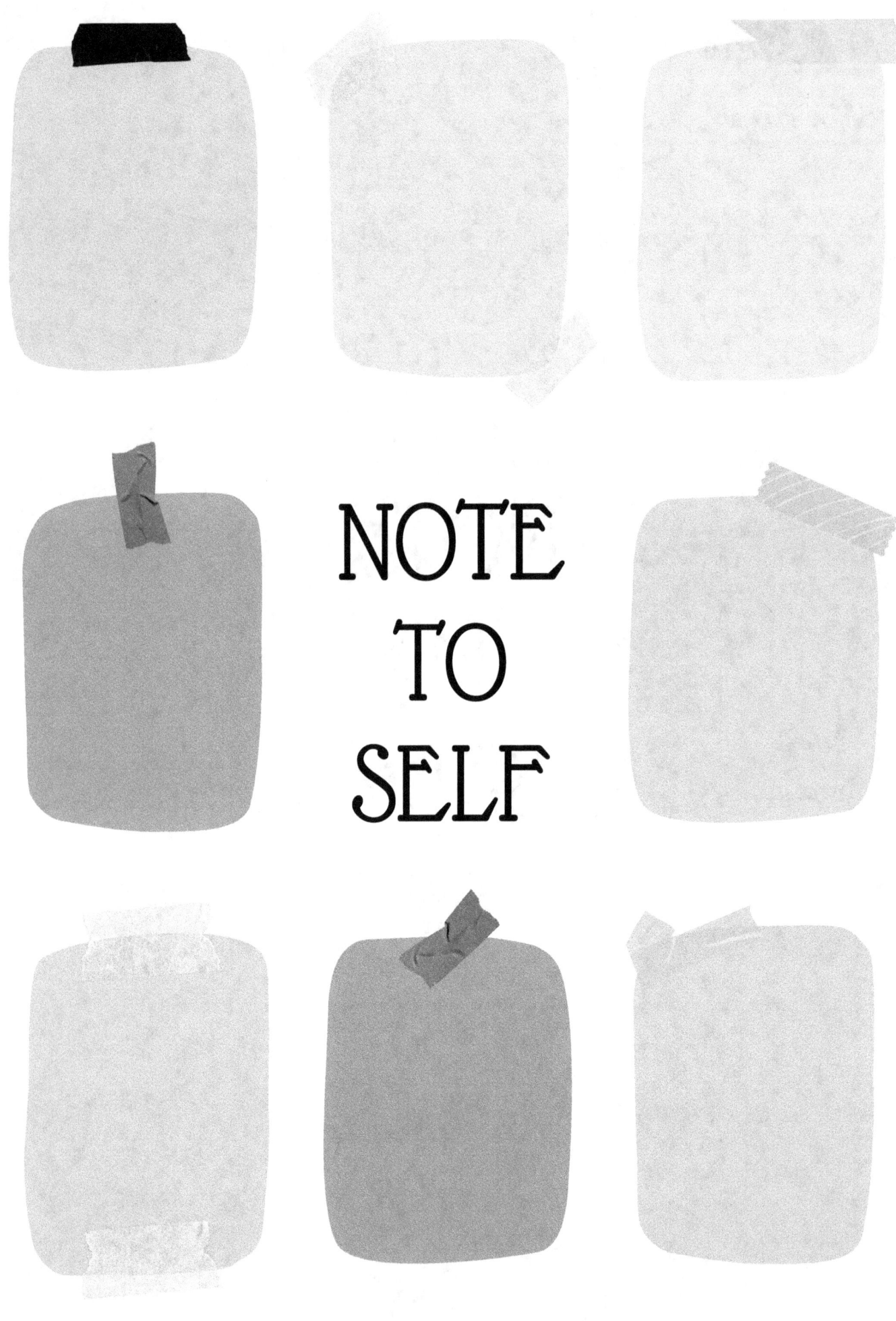

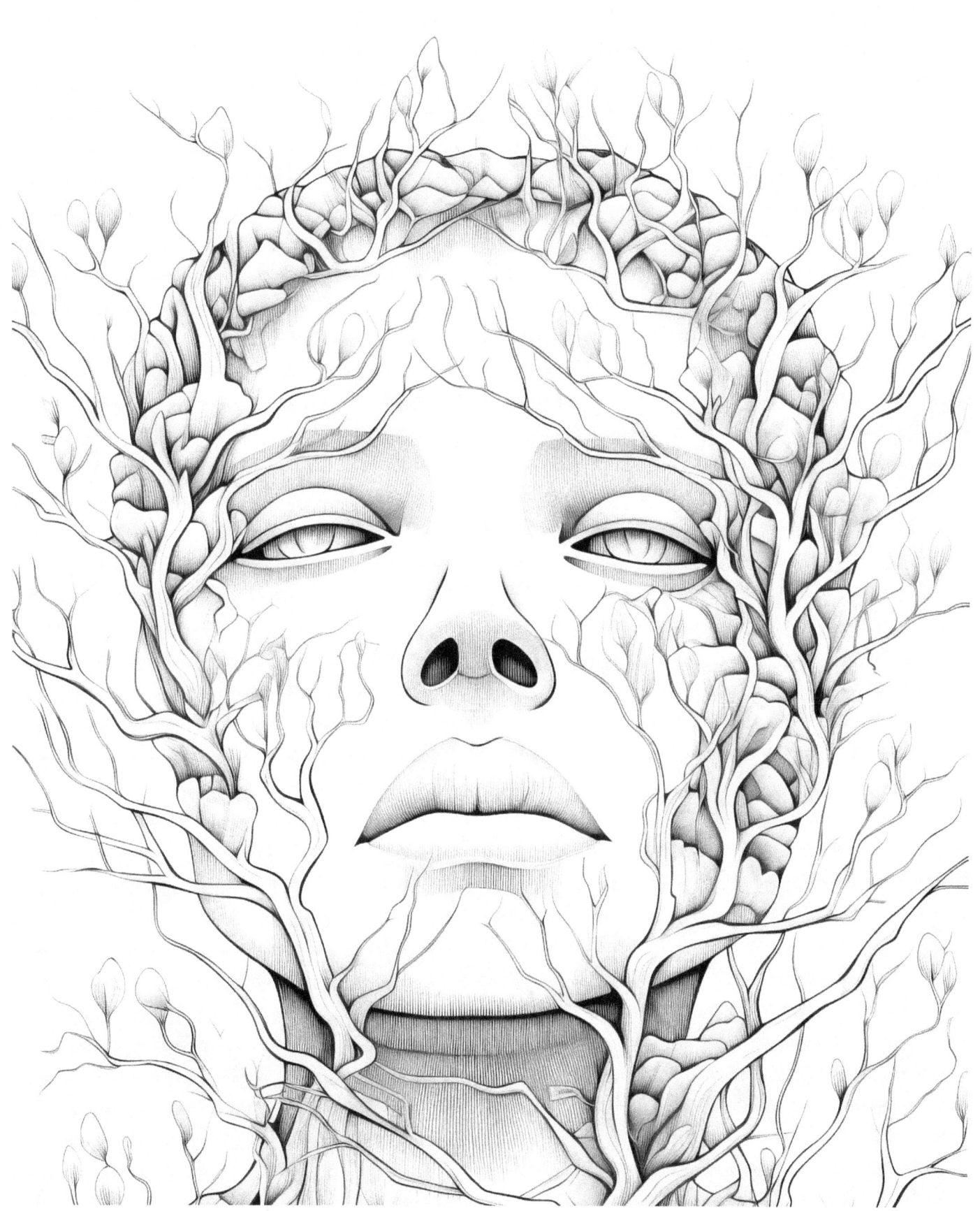

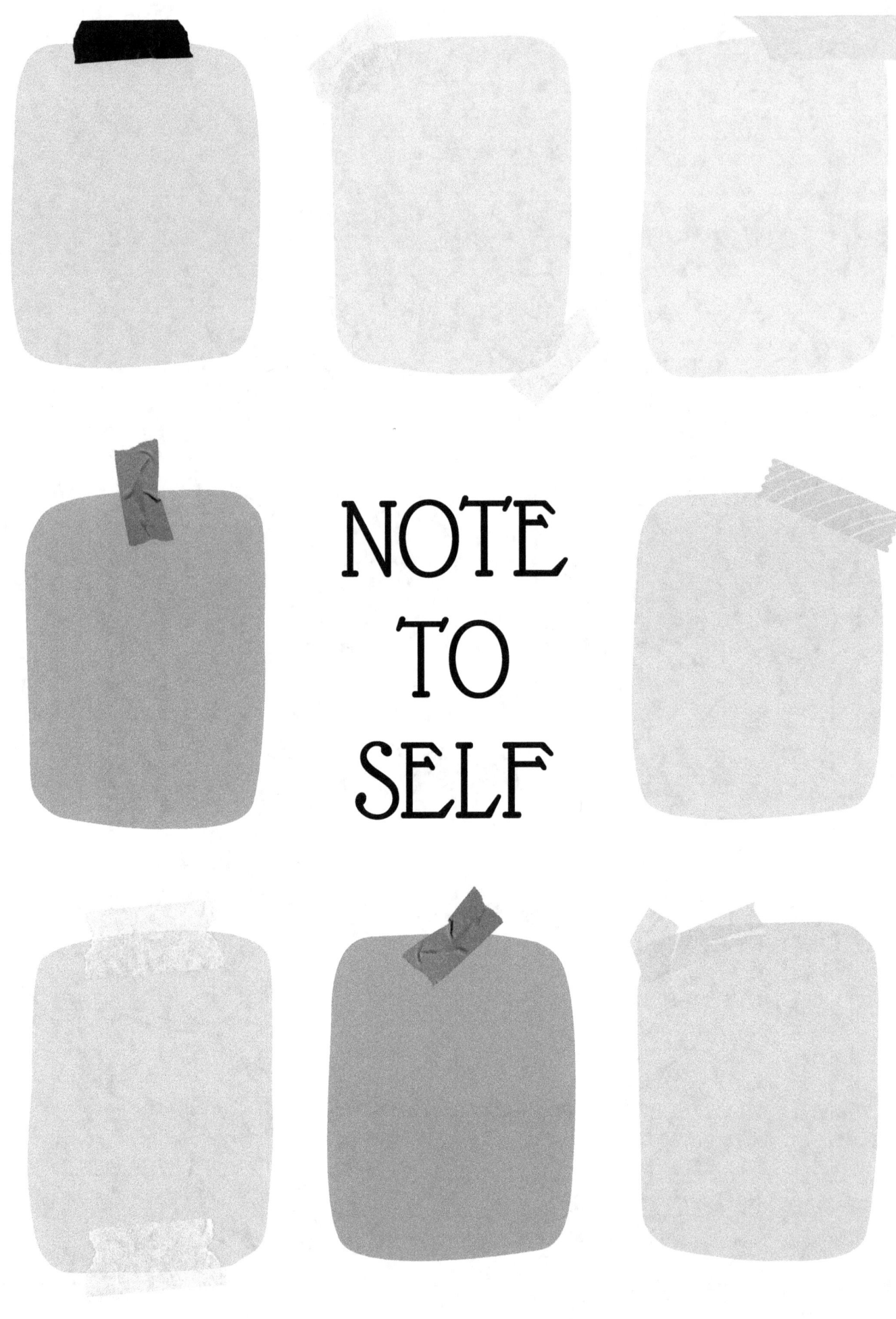

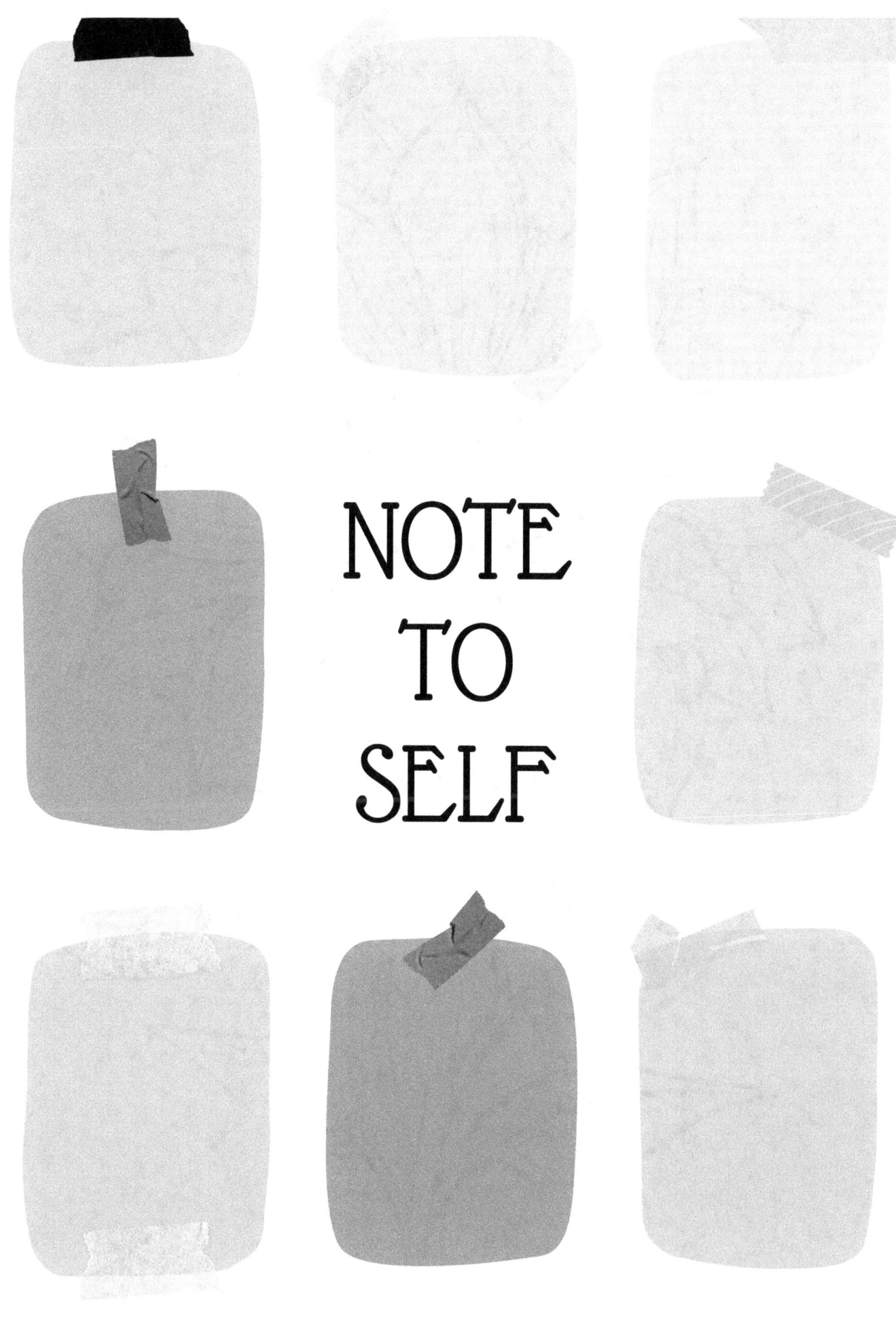

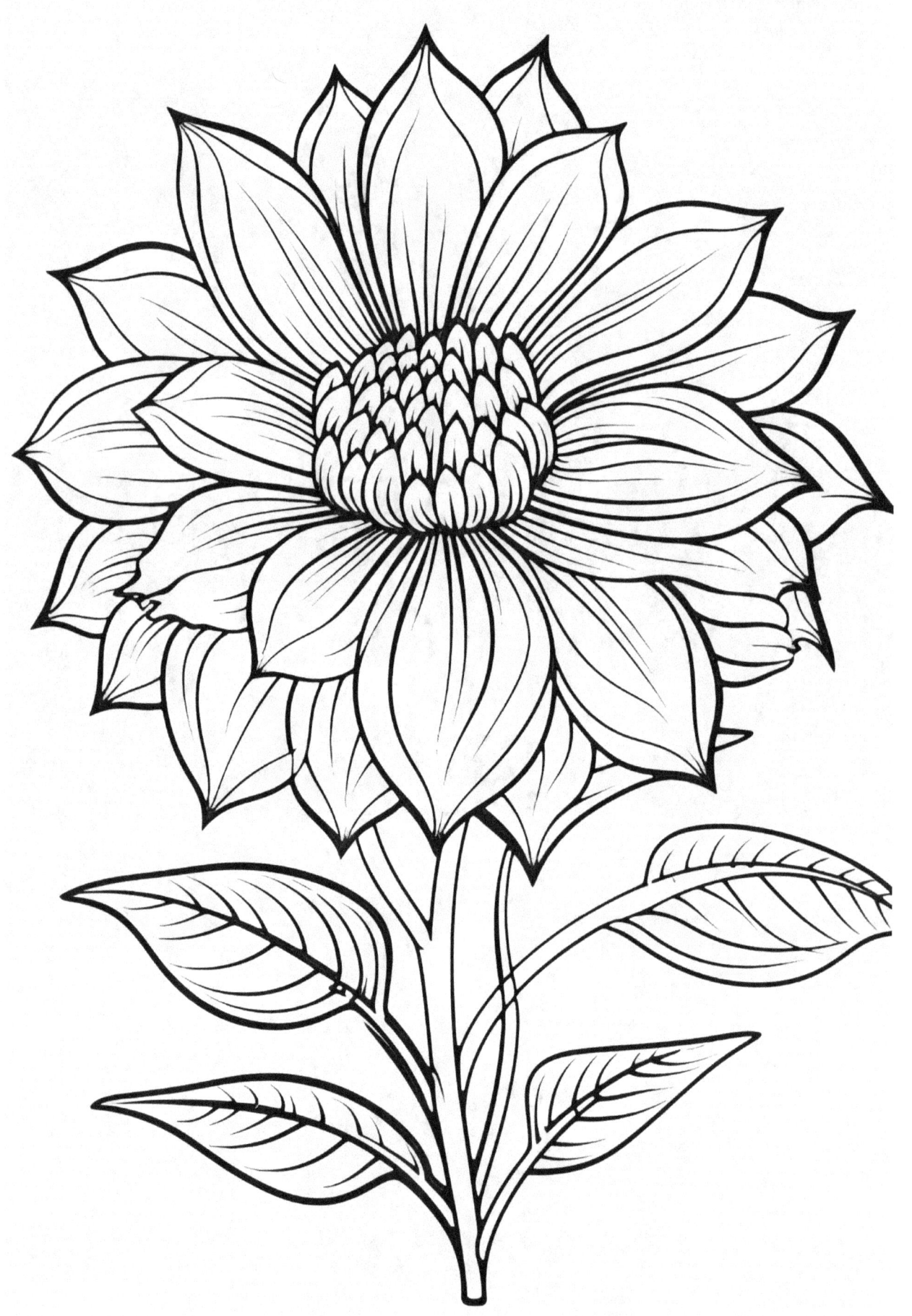

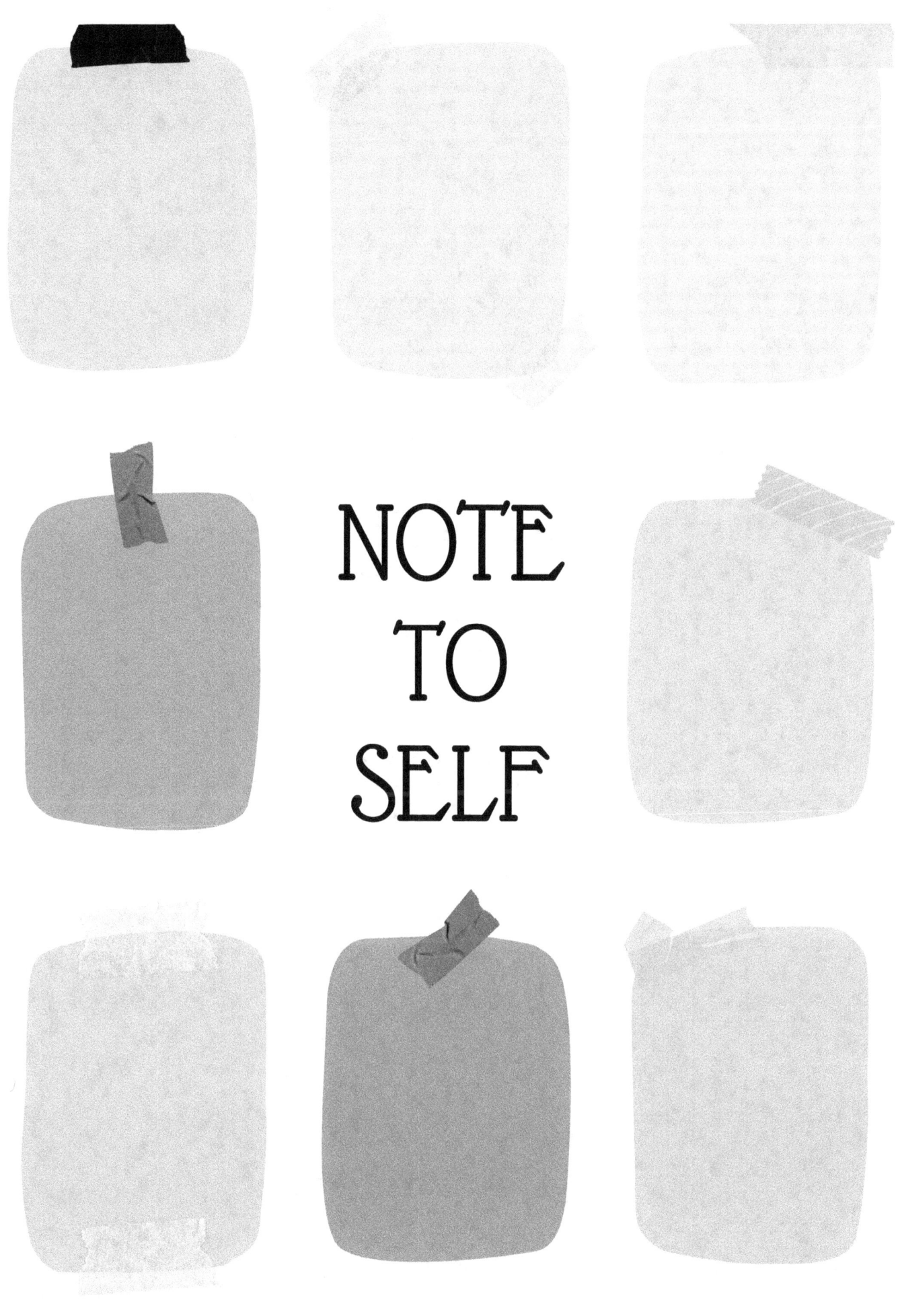

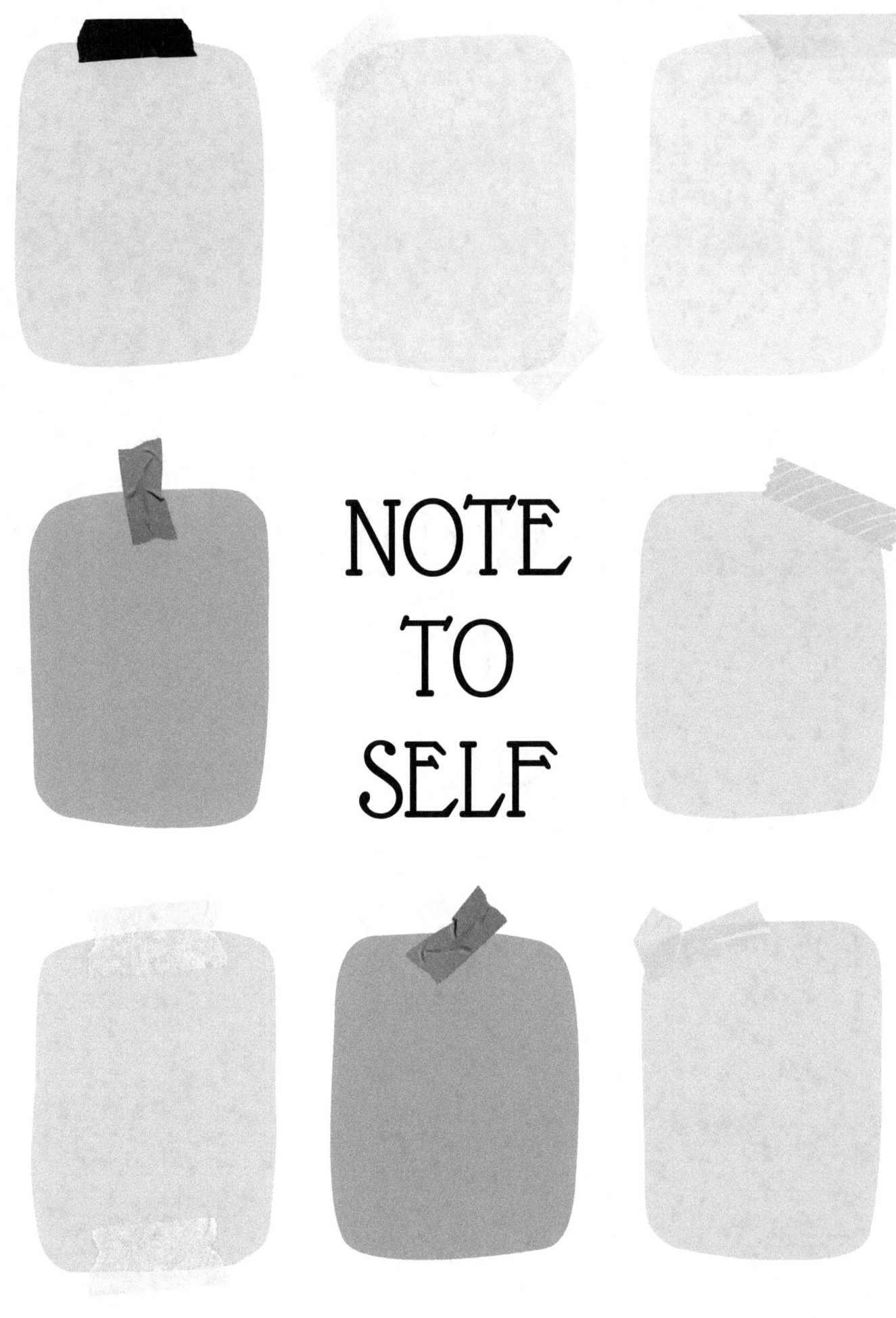

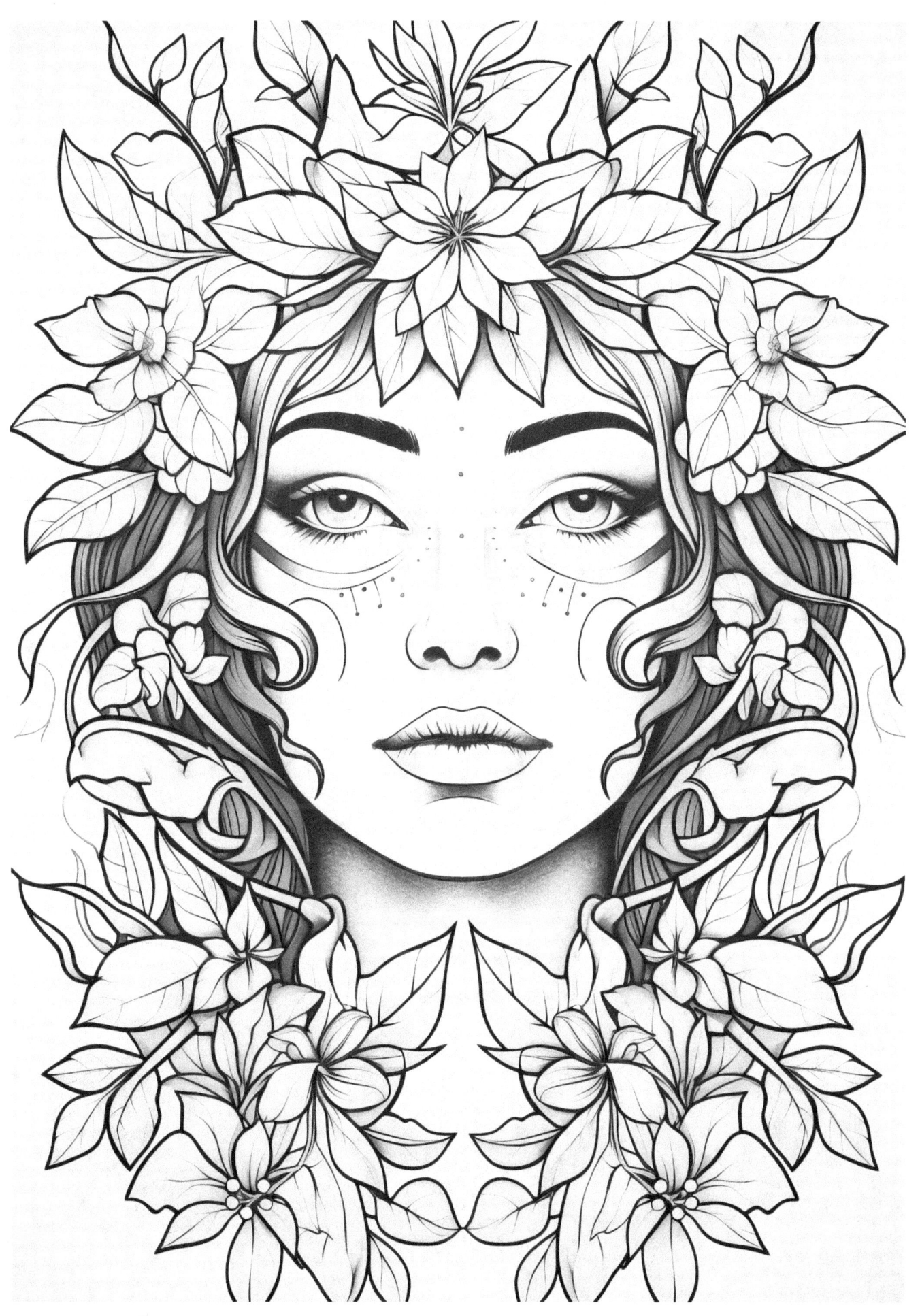

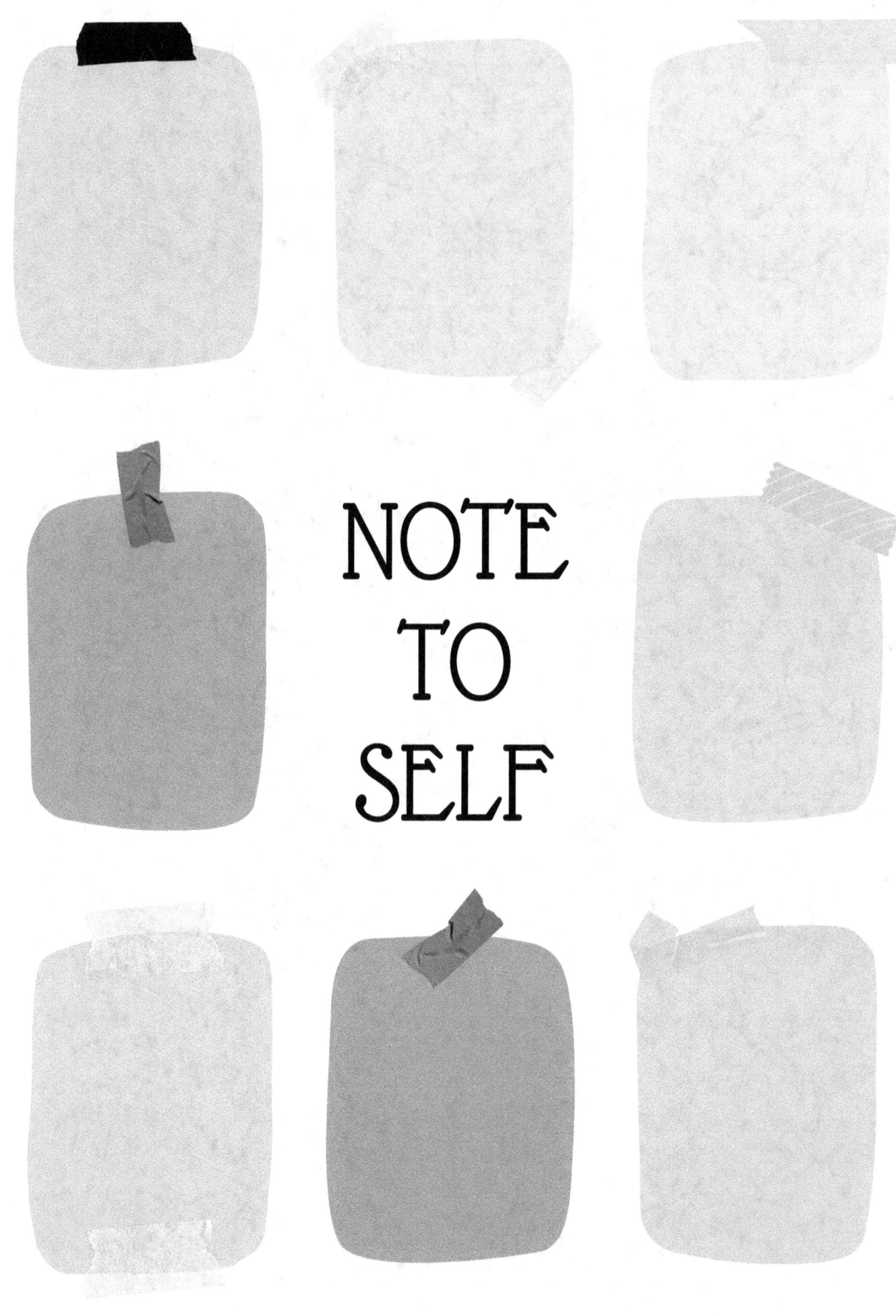

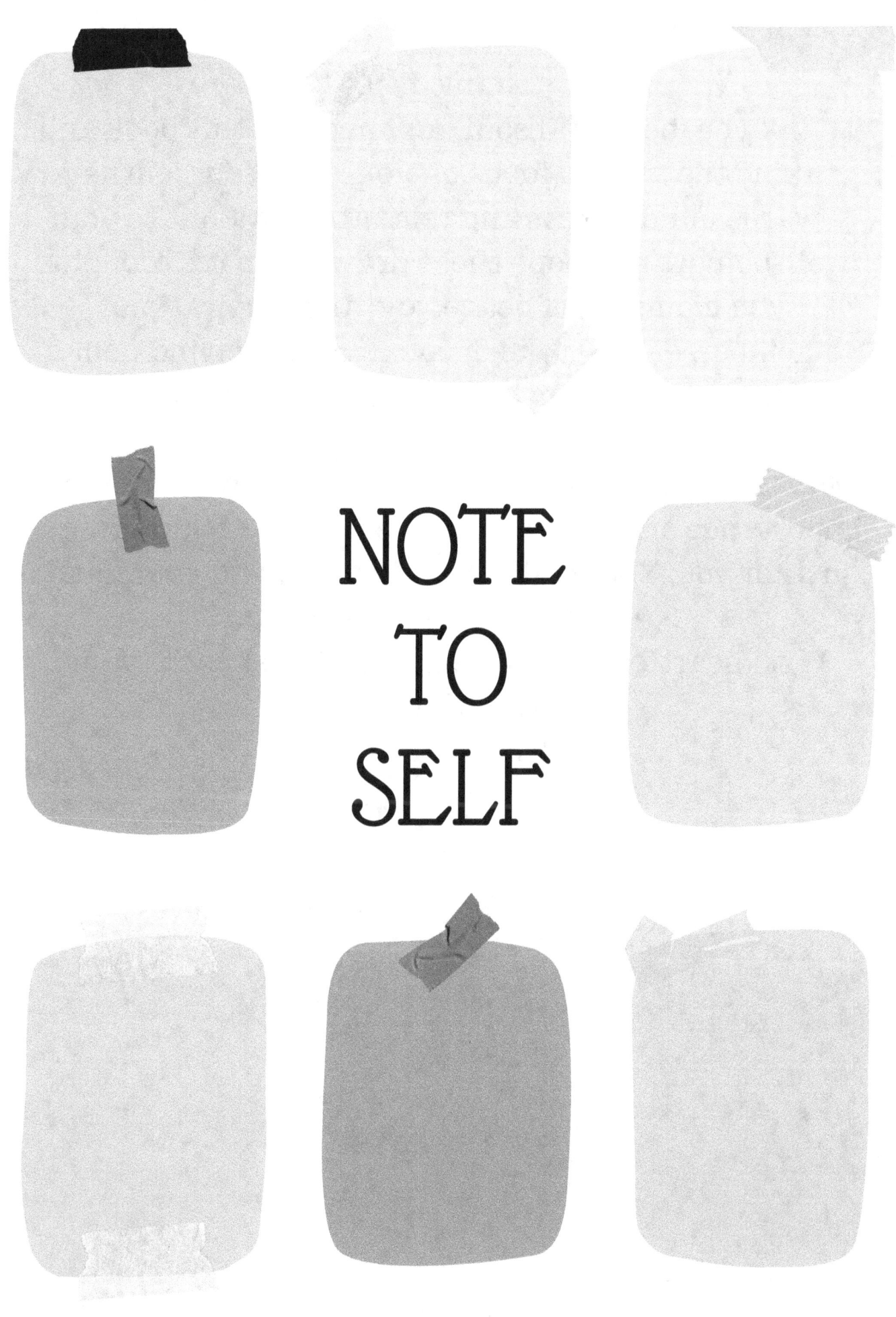

Thank You

Thank you, beautiful soul, for choosing this book and taking the time to focus on yourself. Your journey towards mindfulness and relaxation is a gift to your well-being, and I hope these drawings have brought you moments of peace, joy, and inspiration.

Remember, each stroke of colour and each moment of reflection is a step towards a more mindful and fulfilled you.

May this book continue to serve as a reminder of the importance of self-care and the beauty of taking time just for you. Your dedication to nurturing your mind and spirit is truly inspiring.

With heartfelt gratitude and best wishes for your continued journey,

Orion Windsor

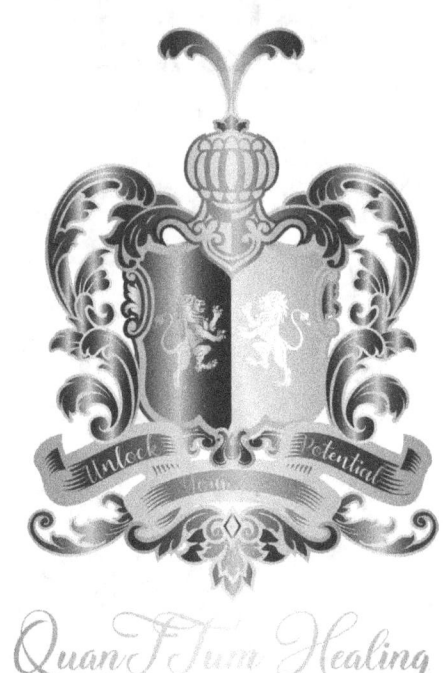